Mental Illness and the Law

Tony Whitehead

Mental Illness and the Law

Basil Blackwell · Oxford

*The names and personal details of all the patients
referred to in this book have been changed to prevent
their identification.*

British Library Cataloguing in Publication Data

Whitehead, Tony
    Mental illness and the law.
    1. Mental health laws — England
    2. Mental health services — England
    I. Title
    344.204'44   KD3412
    ISBN 0-631-12721-6
    ISBN 0-631-12615-5 Pbk

Typesetting by Cambrian Typesetters
Farnborough, Hants
Printed and bound in Great Britain at
The Camelot Press Ltd, Southampton

Contents

Preface

This book is concerned with the laws relating to mental illness and the ways in which they may affect us. To understand the laws it is necessary to know something about mental illness, its treatment and the mental health services, and these subjects will be covered in the early chapters. The greater part of the book, however, will deal with mental health legislation, including the laws on fitness to be tried and to plead, diminished responsibility, testamentary capacity, power of attorney, the Court of Protection and the Mental Health Act of 1959. Two chapters describe the slightly different mental health legislation operating in Scotland and Northern Ireland. Examples of how the law works (or fails to work) will be discussed, and the final chapter will review the whole area.

For the past ten years a number of people and organizations have suggested that the Mental Health Act of 1959 should be amended. In November 1981 the Government published a Mental Health (Amendment) Bill, which contained a number of proposed reforms. This Bill may become law within the next year, so I have outlined the recommendations it contains in the appropriate parts of this book. For many people the Bill does not go far enough, and of course it may be further weakened, or even strengthened, during debate.

My interest in the subject of this book grew out of my work as a psychiatrist and the awareness this brings of society's attitudes to mental illness, as revealed in the various laws relating to the mentally ill and in their interpretation and implementation. Involvement with many people who had disturbed or offended against society, often because of mental illness, showed me the need for a straightforward book which would describe mental illness and the laws bearing upon it for all those who may become involved with the problems that can arise.

The book is intended both for professionals — including solicitors, barristers, magistrates, judges, social workers, doctors and the police — and for the general public, who can easily become ensnared in the complexities of law and medicine. Readers should acquire some basic knowledge about mental illness and come to understand the legal and medical attitudes towards the mentally ill. They will also discover what services exist and learn about the limits of psychiatric treatment, so that they can weigh the resources available against the advantages or disadvantages of drawing on them.

I would like to thank the Controller of Her Majesty's Stationery Office for permission to reproduce the Crown copyright forms in the Appendix.

1 Introduction

'When I use a word,' Humpty Dumpty said in a scornful tone, 'It means just what I choose it to mean – neither more nor less.' Lawyers and psychiatrists are rather like Humpty Dumpty in their tendency to take words we all use and give them special meanings, sometimes known only to themselves. Words like 'assault', 'anxiety', 'depression', 'indecent', 'obsessional', 'hysteria' are all used in everyday conversation, yet when the professionals get hold of them they take on a specific meaning, sometimes quite different from the common usage. Furthermore, the medical and legal professions, like all other trades and occupations, have a jargon of their own which can easily mislead and confuse the uninitiated. The function of language is communication, yet we seem occasionally to delight in depriving language of its ability to convey meaning to other people.

This book is about the law and its relationship to mental illness – an important subject, since any of us might suffer from a mental illness and as a result become involved with the law in some way. Not only does one in ten of the population suffer from an actual mental illness at some time in life, many more are affected by emotional disturbances. As a result they may be at risk, however slight, of becoming involved with the law in its relationship to mental illness, or of doing something that is actually illegal. Involvement with the law is not limited to the 'criminal' and to people who have 'nothing to do with us'; exceeding the speed limit is illegal and so are swearing in public and many other acts that are often done in ignorance of their unlawfulness. So it is useful for everyone to know something about psychiatry and the law in general, and about their interaction in particular.

Solicitors, barristers, magistrates, judges, social workers, probation officers, the police and doctors need not only to know about mental illness and the law, but also to be aware of what is available to the mentally ill in the form of treatment, care, support and accommodation. For example, a judge may have to deal with a case in which the accused is clearly mentally ill; experts will be available to support and enlarge upon the diagnosis, and it may be strongly recommended that the accused should receive treatment. But unless the judge is aware of what treatment is possible and where it is available, he will find it difficult to come to a sensible and humane decision. The term 'treatment' is often bandied around without any explanation of what is actually meant. Some knowledge of psychiatric treatment makes it possible for the right questions to be asked and hence for helpful answers to be obtained.

It is easy to talk about normality, abnormality and mental illness, but difficulties arise when one tries to define the terms. Views and philosophies abound, each with its own definitions, explanations and modes of treatment; to attempt to discuss every theory would inevitably create even greater confusion. To avoid this I shall describe mental illness along orthodox present-day lines, while at the same time pointing out weaknesses in this approach and considering the merits of certain other theories.

2 Mental Handicap and Mental Illness

Everyone seems to know something about mental illness; people call each other 'mad', 'neurotic', 'stupid' and use many other terms that imply mental abnormality. However, when it comes to specifying what is meant by these terms, difficulties immediately arise. I do not intend to begin by defining the concepts of health and mental health; this approach unfortunately creates more difficulties than it solves. There are many definitions of physical health, but none are really satisfactory; even the World Health Organization has failed to come up with an acceptable definition. If it is difficult to describe physical health, describing mental health presents even greater problems. One method of dealing with them is by considering the question of normality and abnormality.

Like madness and its synonyms, normality and abnormality are words in common use, and the people who use them generally have a clear idea of what they mean. A middle-aged city gentleman might describe the behaviour of a teenage football fan as abnormal, implying that he would never dream of donning heavy boots and team hat and scarf and spending a Saturday afternoon screaming abuse at the opposition (in similar garb but of a different colour) and encouragement at his team. Conversely, the teenage football fan might well describe the city gentleman, equipped with bowler hat, umbrella, pin-striped suit and briefcase, in terms that imply abnormality. Thus, one concept of abnormality is 'being different to oneself'. Clearly this view is not very constructive or helpful, yet it is close to one shared by many people, including professionals in the field of mental health. This is the concept of an 'ideal norm', in which the individual is said to be free of 'hang-ups', internal conflict, prejudice and everything else that might interfere with the enjoyment of a full, integrated life governed by intelligence and moral judgement. Of course such paragons do not exist, and even if they did they would be merely moulded in a pattern created by other people. They would also be *ab*normal according to another method of classification. This is the statistical norm, the one we generally use, even when we are not aware we are doing so.

The statistical norm refers to qualities shared by a majority, and can be applied to any human characteristic from height to anxiety level in specific situations. When considering mental abnormality, this is the usual yardstick, but for it to have any meaning or be at all helpful, allowance has to be made for race, culture, education and the general moral values and beliefs of the community involved. Thus it may be statistically normal to believe in witchcraft in certain societies, but abnormal in others. This is to state the obvious, but the fact is sometimes overlooked, particularly since the increase in mobility of people throughout the world, with individuals from one culture settling in others of very different types. Further, it is important to remember that not only may someone from a different culture subscribe to different concepts of morality and belief, but also that such a person may describe symptoms of disease, or other abnormal sensations, in a way that can be so foreign to the culture in which he or she lives that the statements are misunderstood, or even interpreted as the product of a disordered mind. To claim to be possessed by a devil may suggest the presence of mental illness to a psychiatrist unfamiliar with a culture that not only believes in possession, but views certain symptoms as evidence of it.

The statistical norm has not always been the yardstick by which illness has been judged, and even today mistakes are made because of ignorance of what most people do or experience. Until quite recently masturbation was viewed as abnormal, and treatment was prescribed to prevent it. Masturbation is statistically normal, yet the view that it is abnormal still lingers.

One group of mental disorders that has always been defined using the criteria of statistical normality is that now described under the general heading of 'mental handicap'. Before going on to it I should explain a few terms. Mental disorder is an inclusive term that refers to all the categories of mental disability, ranging from mental handicap to psychoses and personality disorders. Mental illness is used to describe a sub-group of mental disorders, which includes psychoses and neuroses and will be described later. Mental handicap forms another sub-group: it is clearly differentiated from mental illness in that it is not an actual illness but an abnormality of intelligence. Usually present from birth, it can also be caused by certain diseases that attack the brain. Many people would consider that mental handicap is not in itself a subject for medical involvement, being more the concern of educators. Other terms that require definition will be described at length under individual subject headings.

Mental handicap

Mental handicap is a term now used to describe what used to be referred to as mental subnormality, and before that, as mental deficiency. Mental handicap, in essence, is a disorder of intelligence, which has been described by W. Stern as 'the general ability to adapt to new situations by means of purposeful thinking'. There are a number of tests used to ascertain intelligence; the result is usually expressed as an intelligence quotient (IQ), a comparison of the mental age, as obtained by testing, with the chronological age. The formula is:

$$IQ = \text{Mental age} \div \text{chronological age} \times 100$$

The idea of mental age is quite clear, but it must be remembered that a person's ability to think does not improve much after the age of sixteen. Thus the formula above is useful only for testing children, since for those over sixteen it would produce declining ratings that fail to describe the true intelligence of the individual. For example, a highly intelligent man with an IQ of 160 at the age of ten might have an IQ as low as fifty when he reached the age of thirty-two. This makes little sense. Consequently one has to make an age correction when calculating the IQ of people over the age of sixteen.

If the intelligence of a large sample of people is measured it is generally found that fifty per cent have an intelligence quotient between seventy and 130, and if the results are plotted on a graph it will have a peak at the 100 level. Thus, those with an IQ below seventy or above 130 are statistically abnormal — having a very high intelligence is just as abnormal as having a very low one, something that is often forgotten. Extremely high intelligence does bring with it many problems, sometimes of such a nature that the highly intelligent individual behaves in a manner which is overtly abnormal and disturbing to others.

An individual with an IQ below seventy is considered to be mentally handicapped. The Mental Health Act of 1959 does not use the intelligence quotient as a method of defining mental handicap or severe mental handicap, but uses the terms subnormality and severe subnormality. Subnormality is defined as:

> a state of arrested or incomplete development of mind (not amounting to severe subnormality), which includes subnormality of intelligence and is of a nature or degree which requires or is susceptible to medical treatment or other special care or training of the patient.

Severe subnormality is defined as:

> a state of arrested or incomplete development of mind which includes subnormality of intelligence and is of such a nature or degree that the patient is incapable of living an independent life or of guarding himself against serious exploitation, or will be so incapable when of an age to do so.

Thus the mentally handicapped individual has a low intelligence of a degree that necessitates special training, while someone who is severely handicapped is so disabled that he or she is unable to live an independent life and always requires the help and support of people of normal intelligence.

The Mental Health (Amendment) Bill suggests that the terms subnormality and severe subnormality used in the principal Act be changed to mental handicap and severe mental handicap. It also proposes new definitions of these conditions:

> In this Act 'severe mental handicap' means a state of arrested, or incomplete development of mind, which includes severe impairment of intelligence and social functioning.

In this Act 'mental handicap' means a state of arrested, or incomplete development of mind (not amounting to severe mental handicap), which includes significant impairment of intelligence and social functioning.

Mentally handicapped individuals can and do live normal, full lives, but many are easily influenced by others and a few commit offences, either because of this influence, or because they do not understand that what they are doing is illegal. Here the measure of mental age is perhaps more useful and comprehensible than the intelligence quotient, since it seems to give a clearer picture of the individual's ability and understanding of the law. But it can be misleading; tests of intelligence are not infallible, and if a man has a mental age of perhaps eight when in fact he is thirty-five, this does not mean that he is simply an overgrown eight-year-old. Ageing brings with it an improved understanding of life and an increase in knowledge whether the individual is mentally handicapped, of normal intelligence, or a genius. Intelligence testing cannot reveal all these factors, but it is still a useful guide to an individual's ability to manage independently and survive in the real world. The point I am trying to make is that while mental handicap does diminish a person's responsibility, it is important to assess each individual fully before coming to any conclusion, rather than simply taking an IQ rating as evidence of an individual's ability to manage independently, or degree of his or her self-reliance.

Intelligence is inherited, but it can be affected by environmental factors. Where inheritance of intelligence is concerned, the phenomenon known as deviation towards the mean needs to be taken into account. This means that through a number of generations there is a tendency for particular characteristics, such as intelligence, to move towards normality. Parents with low intelligence tend to have children a little more intelligent than they are, while highly intelligent parents tend to have children with slightly lower intelligence than themselves. I make this point to dispel the not uncommon fear that people of low intelligence produce extremely unintelligent children. This myth has caused considerable misery in the past, causing mentally handicapped individuals to be incarcerated and isolated from members of the opposite sex.

The majority of mentally handicapped individuals simply have a lower intelligence than normal, without any specific cause. However there are specific conditions that can cause mental handicap, severe mental handicap in particular. There may be damage to the foetus while it is still in the womb, or to the baby during the process of birth, or by disease after birth. Diseases of the mother may affect the child; German measles and syphilis are two well-known examples. The use of tobacco and alcohol by the pregnant mother or the effects of irradiation may harm the foetus. There are also a number of specific disorders that cause mental handicap, such as the following:

Tuberous sclerosis (epiloia)
Tumours develop in the brain and other parts of the body. Epilepsy is usually present in early childhood and may persist throughout life. The degree of mental handicap is often very severe.

Microcephaly
In this condition the skull has a much smaller circumference than normal. The victim is often severely mentally handicapped because the brain tissue is compressed, or is unable to develop inside the small skull. Epilepsy is common and the facial features tend to be birdlike, with the nose assuming undue prominence as a result of the size and shape of the head. This condition may be inherited or produced by irradiation of the foetus.

Phenylketonuria
The result of a biochemical disturbance in which the body is unable to break down certain proteins consumed as food, producing a poison which retards the development of brain and other body tissue. The sufferer is usually small, with fair hair and blue eyes. This condition can be prevented provided that a diagnosis is made early in the child's life and a special diet is prescribed. The condition can be diagnosed with a simple urine test.

Cretinism
This condition is due to a deficiency of the thyroid hormone and can be effectively treated by giving thyroid extract as soon as possible after birth.

Down's Syndrome
Down's Syndrome used to be called mongolism, since sufferers have a superficial facial resemblance to Mongolians. In addition they often suffer from congenital abnormalities: umbilical hernias, shortened little fingers, fissured tongues and gruff voices. Mental handicap is always present, though the degree can vary considerably; some sufferers have only mild impairment. The condition is caused by a gross chromosomal abnormality and is related to the age of the mother and/or father: older parents are the most likely to produce children with Down's Syndrome.

Help for the mentally handicapped
Mental handicap itself does not require treatment in a medical sense, nor should it receive it. Many handicapped children can be educated in normal schools provided they are given some extra assistance. Some people argue that all mentally handicapped children should be educated in normal schools, but that is not the case at present. Special education in special schools is available and there are training centres and occupational centres for older mentally handicapped people. The severely mentally handicapped may require a considerable amount of care, and there may be medical problems since severe mental handicap is often accompanied by gross physical abnormalities.

The roles of medicine and psychiatry in providing help for the mentally handicapped lie in assessing and diagnosing the conditions that may respond to treatment, and, in the case of psychiatry, in providing help for any associated emotional problems that may occur.

Mental illness: the psychoses

Mental illnesses can be categorized in varous ways; the usual method is to describe three or four main groups. These are the psychoses, the neuroses, personality disorders and organic brain disease. The term organic brain disease covers all those mental conditions caused by actual physical changes in or damage to the brain. Personality disorder is a classification which covers a multitude of behavioural problems, and will be discussed in detail in chapter 3. The neuroses and the psychoses are the two major groups of mental illness. In the past it was thought that a mentally ill person who was obviously abnormal but unaware of it was most likely to be suffering from a psychosis, while someone who was conscious of suffering from an emotional disorder was likely to be suffering from a neurosis. 'Insight' appeared to be the crucial differentiating factor, but in fact this is not so: individuals who are suffering from one of the psychoses often realize there is something wrong, while many victims of neurosis do not believe their problems are emotional and may strongly deny such a suggestion. One way of discussing the psychoses is to describe the individual conditions and so avoid arguments about definition. On the whole the psychoses are the more serious types of mental illness and reveal themselves in behaviour that is obviously extraordinary to any objective observer.

The psychoses consist of schizophrenia (or rather the schizophrenias), severe or endogenous depression, mania and hypomania. There is also puerperal psychosis, which afflicts women around the period of childbirth, but this is not a true category since it is made up of a variety of different illnesses, as will be explained later.

Schizophrenia
Schizophrenia is the major psychosis in that it accounts for the greatest number of young and middle-aged people in mental hospitals. There is considerable debate about the nature and origins of schizophrenia. Some consider that it is simply an individual's reaction to an intolerable life situation, while others, taking the opposite extreme, believe that it is an illness produced by abnormal chemical changes in the brain. Again, there is evidence that a tendency to schizophrenia can be inherited, but a tendency only; studies of identical twins have shown that one twin can develop schizophrenia without

the other automatically following suit. It is perhaps best, because of all this confusion as to origin, to talk about the schizophrenias, using the plural to suggest that the condition may have many different origins.

To illustrate this point it is worth taking an example from general medicine. In the past, people were diagnosed as suffering from dropsy when they developed swelling of the legs, abdomen or other parts of the body due to the retention of fluid. When digitalis was first used as a treatment for this condition it was found that some patients improved while others did not. We know now that oedema, another word for dropsy, can be caused by many different conditions, from heart and kidney disease to malnutrition. It was the cases caused by heart disease that tended to improve when given digitalis. Schizophrenia today is in much the same position as dropsy was in the past, and our understanding of its origins is as primitive as was our understanding of the causes of dropsy. Present treatment is a little like the rather hit-and-miss method of using digitalis long ago.

One common mistake is to translate schizophrenia as 'split mind'. In fact, schizophrenia means a fragmentation of the mind, while 'split mind' is a colloquial way of describing the 'Doctor Jekyll and Mr Hyde' phenomenon. There are not many Jekyll and Hydes around, but there are people who have two or more separate personalities and change from one to another in a dramatic way. This is a neurotic reaction and has nothing to do with schizophrenia. It appears to be subject to fashion, having been more common in the past than it is at present. Schizophrenia used to be called dementia praecox; the modern word for the illness was coined in 1911 by Eugen Bleuler, a Swiss psychiatrist. He considered that an important feature of the condition was a fragmentation of mental functions, with thought being split off from emotion and itself divided up in various ways.

To confuse the issue further, schizophrenia is split up into a number of sub-groups. There have been various classifications, one originated by Bleuler, who talked of simple, hebephrenic, catatonic and paranoid schizophrenia. His categorization is no longer much in use, since its significance and value are in doubt. Many sufferers may present a picture of simple schizophrenia at one time and later show symptoms of the other types. There will be a further brief discussion of these terms below.

Certain symptoms of schizophrenia are present in the sufferer in various combinations: withdrawal from social contact; disturbed and fragmented thinking, which may include the coining of new words (neologisms); facial grimacing; muttering; outbursts of purposeless laughter; and the inappropriate expression of emotion. A woman might laugh at events which would normally cause her to feel sad. But we are looking here at the expression of emotion; despite her laughter, the woman's actual feelings may be of sadness. There may be a lack of emotional contact, the 'glass wall' phenomenon. You can see the patient but you cannot 'reach' him.

The victim of schizophrenia may believe that his thoughts are being stolen, or that his thoughts and actions are being controlled by some external force, or that chance events have been deliberately planned to affect him in some deeply personal way. Many schizophrenics believe that people on the radio or television are talking about them. This is an example of a delusion, a mistaken belief that would not be held by other people in the patient's immediate social group or in the wider society, and that is not susceptible to reasoned argument. Delusions can occur in many mental disorders.

The delusions that occur in schizophrenia are of two main types: those that apparently spring out of nowhere, and those that, to the patient, make sense of bizarre experiences that cannot otherwise be explained. Some psychiatrists call the first type an unsystematized delusion; to take an example, a previously normal man awoke one morning with the sudden conviction that he was to be elected as president. The second type of delusion, the systematized delusion, is exemplified by a man who, having felt that his thoughts were being stolen, built up a complex system of delusional explanations to account for this, including the beliefs that he was a genius and the reincarnation of Christ. Delusions vary enormously, ranging from a conviction that you are someone other than yourself, to imagining that you are the victim of plots and other abuses.

Schizophrenics may also experience hallucinations. A

hallucination is a perception or sensory experience without any detectable basis in external reality. Hallucinations may affect hearing, vision, smell or touch, but in schizophrenia they are usually auditory. Like delusions, hallucinations can occur in many mental disorders, including those of physical origin, such as acute toxic confusion (see chapter 3).

Disturbances of thinking may occur in a number of ways. One quite common symptom of thought disorder is called 'knight's move': the individual's thoughts jump from one idea to the next in a tangential manner, like the L-shaped move of the knight in chess. Some patients complain of thoughts reverberating inside their heads, a symptom called 'thought resonance' or thought echoing. 'Thought blocking' may occur; here a sequence of thought comes to a halt abruptly as if it has run up against a brick wall. The patient may describe this condition, or it may be observed when speaking to a patient who suddenly stops in mid-sentence for no apparent reason.

The following brief descriptions of the different sub-categories of schizophrenia illustrate other symptoms of the illness and at the same time explain what is meant by the terms, which are still occasionally used, though no longer so highly regarded.

Catatonic schizophrenia is a condition in which the patient goes into a stupor, possibly remaining immobile for hours on end. While in this state the patient's arms and legs can be moved into odd positions which are then maintained. The term 'waxy flexibility' is used to describe the condition of the limbs; they feel as if they are made of stiff plasticine. Following an attack of stupor the patient may become extremely overactive and destructive.

Catatonic stupor was frequently seen in the past but is now, for some reason, a rarity. Early treatment cannot be the reason: many catatonics in the past have complained to me for the first time with this symptom, so as nothing was wrong before they could hardly have been treated prior to the stupor.

Other symptoms of catatonic schizophrenia are echolalia, in which the patient repeats word for word anything that is said to him, and echopraxia, when he will mimic other people's actions.

Paranoid schizophrenia is typified by the development of persecutory delusions, in which patients believe that other people are plotting against them and acting so as to cause them distress.

Hebephrenic schizophrenia is typified by rather silly, exaggerated, adolescent behaviour, marked by guilt and concern about sexual matters.

Simple schizophrenia usually involves a gradual withdrawal from society, with much preoccupation with oneself and a loss of emotional expression, or 'flattening of affect'.

Schizophrenia can thus take many forms: some individuals develop a single type, while others suffer the whole range of symptoms. Schizophrenia may occur as an isolated attack followed by complete recovery, or it may recur, or it may become a long, progressive, chronic illness. Recovery can happen without treatment or other intervention; even when the patient is treated it is often difficult to know whether this has genuinely been effective or has simply coincided with a change in the patient's condition.

Treatment   The orthodox treatment of schizophrenia consists of prescribing certain drugs, such as chlorpromazine (Largactil), trifluoperazine (Stelazine), fluphenazine (Moditen and Modecate), or flupenthixol (Depixol). The last two preparations can be given as long-acting, intramuscular injections. Drug treatment is combined with a programme of rehabilitation, both social and occupational. This is not the only way of treating schizophrenia; some psychiatrists consider that it responds to psychotherapy, while others would advocate the therapeutic community approach discussed in chapter 4. The chief consideration in the treatment of schizophrenia, as with any other mental illness, is to ensure that the action taken does not make the patient's condition worse. One danger is that if you confine a patient in an institution, you expose him or her to the risks of institutionalism, or institutional neurosis, a disease in its own right.

The affective psychoses

The term 'affective psychoses' encompasses those mental

disorders in which the mood of the sufferer appears to be seriously affected. The most common type is depression in its various guises.

The word 'depression' means different things to different people; it can describe states ranging from being merely 'fed up' to suffering from such despair that death seems to be the only solution. In psychiatry, four broad categories of depression are identified. First, there is what could be called normal depression, typically arising from grief and bereavement. Many people think it important that this should not be considered as an illness or a subject for psychiatric intervention; this is not to say that people who are grieving over loss do not need help and support, but they should never be classified as mentally ill and certainly never given physical treatments using antidepressants, tranquillizers or electroconvulsive therapy (ECT). People 'in grief' can behave abnormally, can even fall foul of the law as a result. I will examine this subject, along with the two other types of depression, neurotic and reactive, in chapter 3. Here I want to discuss the fourth type of depression, variously described as severe, endogenous or psychotic depression.

Severe depression
Orthodox psychiatrists view this condition as something that arises within the individual in the absence of any apparent external precipitating factor, suggesting that it is likely to be a biochemical rather than a psychological disorder. This view is not universally accepted, however, and many believe that severe depression is simply a more extreme form of the other types of depression. At present there seems to be no way of resolving this conflict of ideas on its origin, but it is possible to discuss what is meant by severe depression and what can be done to alleviate it.

Severe depression can be divided into a number of sub-categories such as agitated depression, retarded depression, involutionary depression and senile depression. But on the whole these sub-categories are not particularly helpful, and certainly the term senile depression is not just unhelpful, but offensive, meaning only that this depression occurs in elderly patients.

The symptoms of severe depression include a personal sense of misery and worthlessness, frequently associated with profound and needless guilt. The sufferer dreads the future because everything seems hopeless, and often thinks of death as the only escape. Sleep disturbances are common – sufferers often tend to wake up early in the morning and then be unable to go to sleep again. In severe depression, the mornings are the worst time of the day. Another symptom is a reduction in appetite – many of the more severely affected patients refuse to eat at all. There is a loss of interest in both work and self, and a general slowing down of all physical and mental activity; this can progress to a state of stupor, where the patient may simply sit in a chair all day, doing and saying nothing, but with a facial expression of deep sadness. Depressive stupor is the final stage of the condition called retarded depression. It differs from schizophrenic stupor in that there is no waxy flexibility of the limbs and the victim's appearance is unmistakably severely depressed. Sometimes the depressed person exhibits considerable restlessness, wandering around, fidgeting, picking things up and putting them down and performing other aimless activities. This condition, sometimes called agitated depression, is always characterized by a bizarre combination of much pointless activity coupled with a slowing down of purposeful thought and action.

Loss of sexual interest and activity is another symptom, illustrating the error of the commonly held belief that mental illness is associated with an increase in sexual drive. Victims of the two major psychoses – endogenous depression and schizophrenia – have to add to all their other suffering a loss of the happiness that people gain from sexual activity. Psychotic depression, in fact, takes away all the pleasures from life and replaces them with misery, apathy and despair.

Symptoms of anxiety are not uncommon, and may include an unjustified feeling of fear, palpitations, a dryness of the mouth, sweating (particularly of the palms), tight sensations in the head, chest and abdomen, breathlessness, frequent passing of urine, muscular weakness, tremor of the hands and faintness. These symptoms may convince victims that they have some serious physical illness, and in turn can confuse doctors into believing that patients are suffering from heart disease, respiratory problems or other organic disorders.

Some victims of severe depression experience hallucinations and develop delusional beliefs. The hallucinations are usually auditory and always unpleasant. Patients may hear people saying distressing things about them, such as accusing them of being prostitutes, murderers or thieves. They may hear threats against their life, or the voices of children or relatives crying out in pain as though they are being tortured. The delusional beliefs are also disagreeable, although they can sometimes be rather grandiose, like those of one man who believed he was infected with a virulent strain of syphilis that would spread throughout the world and destroy all human life.

Involutional depression, or involutional melancholia, is severe depression occurring in middle age. Traditionally the terms were applied solely to women near the menopause, but in fact middle-aged men can develop a similar condition. Involutional depression is typified by agitation, hallucinations and unpleasant delusions.

One relatively rare but important type of severe depression is known as hidden or smiling depression. Here the sufferer is physically and mentally depressed, but denies it and may even be able to raise a weak smile. People with this type of depression tend to complain only of the physical symptoms, so they may undergo extensive investigations for physical diseases before it is realized that they are depressed.

Victims of severe depression may commit suicide or kill others, though the latter is rare, and invariably involves near relatives: a severely depressed husband perhaps might kill his wife and children to protect them from the horrors of life. Nonetheless, it is important to bear in mind that the great majority of sufferers do not endanger other people and only harm themselves if there is a failure to provide help and treatment at an early stage in the illness.

Treatment   The orthodox treatment of severe depression is to administer antidepressant drugs, such as amitriptyline (Tryptizol) or mianserin (Norval, Bolvidon), use electro-convulsive therapy, or combine the two. Most patients respond quickly to these forms of treatment provided they are combined with a degree of psychotherapy and counselling, and, if appropriate, social manipulation. Treatment will be considered in more depth in chapter 4, but I must emphasize here that most mental disorders demand a number of different approaches, and in the case of depression, help needs to be provided promptly, effectively and humanely.

Mania and hypomania

Less common than depression is another psychotic condition that is primarily concerned with mood and that could be considered the converse of depression. This is called 'mania' in its more severe form and 'hypomania' in its more common and less serious stage of development. Many people regard mania as simply another word for madness, but in technical usage mania is applied to a specific type of illness. Sufferers are elated, overactive and full of hope and a sense of well-being, and they often express grand plans for the future. There is usually a great flow of talk that tends to jump from one subject to another, but always in a connected way. Often sufferers have grandiose delusions about their physical and mental powers.

Sleep may be disturbed because patients are so active and involved with their remarkable plans that they have no time for rest, and as a result they may become physically exhausted. Appetite is not affected, but, again because of the frenzied activity, meals may be taken irregularly and sometimes missed completely. In spite of these general feelings of elation and happiness, sufferers can quickly become angry if their plans are thwarted, though fortunately the anger quickly evaporates if one changes the subject to something neutral or more cheerful. Distractibility is one of the symptoms of mania and can be used as a method of dealing with a patient who is becoming increasingly difficult to deal with or angry.

Treatment   As with depression, it is important to provide treatment for mania as quickly as possible, since the victim can not only be socially disruptive, but also get into difficulties caused by the grandiose delusions. Phenomenal debts can be incurred; impossible contracts made; and real or imaginary fortunes lost overnight. One patient I knew tried to offer his services to the Palestine Liberation Organization during one attack of hypomania, and in the next offered his imagined military brilliance to the Israelis.

The first step in orthodox treatment is to use one of the major tranquillizers, such as chlorpromazine (Largactil), or, more commonly, haloperidol (Serenace). Lithium carbonate has been used successfully during the past few years not only to deal with mania attacks, but also as a preventative measure. It is also used in the treatment of recurrent severe depressions, though it is not so effective here. Again, some degree of psychological intervention, help and support is also necessary, particularly when medication has already produced some degree of calming.

Manic depressive psychoses
Some psychiatrists diagnose all victims of severe depression or mania as suffering from a manic depressive psychosis. Whether this is legitimate or not, there certainly do exist people who suffer from attacks of both severe depression and mania, and some swing from one to the other with only brief periods of normality in between. Sometimes the illness presents itself as a simultaneous mixture of depression and mania: this is relatively rare and can make diagnosis very difficult. For instance, one patient claimed he had grown the largest marrow in the world and then, with a tear in his eye, said: 'But that bastard next door has stolen it.' Here we have a grandiose delusion followed by a depressive delusion with a paranoid flavour, which might suggest a diagnosis of schizophrenia. This however would be both incorrect and unhelpful as far as treatment is concerned. Old people are more likely to develop this strange jumbled outlook than any other age group.

Puerperal psychoses
The term puerperal psychosis is applied to a psychotic illness occurring in a woman at the time of childbirth or shortly after. In the past, infections and other toxic conditions were quite common consequences of childbirth and produced acute and sub-acute toxic confusional states. (These will be

considered in chapter 3.) This is now extremely rare, but some women do develop severe depression at childbirth, and others may experience an acute schizophrenic attack. Still others may develop various types of neurotic reaction to pregnancy and childbirth. Thus a puerperal psychosis or neurosis is simply a psychotic or neurotic illness occurring around the period of childbirth. Clearly these illnesses must be related in some way to the pregnancy and birth, but this relationship is often difficult to explore and evaluate. The illnesses do respond well to treatment, but can be accompanied by special problems and, of course, by the fear of a recurrence if the woman becomes pregnant again. One serious problem is that of the woman who kills her child because of severe depression, schizophrenia or other emotional reaction. This syndrome has been recognized since ancient times, and is covered by special legislation.

This brief description of the psychoses has illustrated the different types of serious mental illness. It is important to remember that most victims of these illnesses respond to treatment and do not cause any major social problems; only a small proportion actually harm themselves or others. The majority will either seek and obtain treatment of their own free will, or accept treatment when it is offered, or manage without it. A few people may develop an illness to such a degree that the use of compulsory powers may be necessary, either to protect them from themselves, or, much less commonly, to protect others.

I shall consider the question of compulsory admission to hospital in detail in chapter 5, but it must be mentioned here that having a psychotic illness does not in itself warrant the use of compulsory powers when someone refuses professional help. Our knowledge of mental illness and what is normal and abnormal is insufficient to justify professional intervention simply because a professional states that someone is suffering from schizophrenia or some other condition and in his opinion must be treated. The liberty of the individual is much too important to allow such professional arrogance, particularly when one remembers that treatment is based on empiricism, cannot be guaranteed to work and is sometimes carried out in institutions that inflict more harm than good. It is best to confine the use of compulsion to those who are without a doubt a danger to themselves or to others.

In the next chapter I shall examine the neuroses and that difficult medical, social and legal problem, the personality disorder.

3 More about Mental Illness

The neuroses

It is common practice to group together a whole range of conditions under the general heading of neuroses and personality disorders. Included in this category are a variety of abnormalities of personality, such as extreme suspiciousness, excessive aggressiveness, sexual deviance and the abuse of alcohol or drugs. However, to lump all these conditions together as personality disorders, as some authorities would recommend, can be rather misleading. There is little in common between the person who suffers from an obsessional compulsive neurosis and the aggressively anti-social psychopath, except that they are both abnormal by prevailing social standards.

The most obvious difference between a patient with a neurosis or personality disorder and one with a psychosis is that the neurotic is likely to behave in a way that is, if not necessarily quite like everyone else, at least understandable to normal people. A neurotic person's behaviour is an exaggeration of the way most of us behave at some time or other, without suspecting that we have a mental illness. An acutely ill psychotic person usually behaves in a way that is outside the experience of most of us; we find his or her behaviour difficult to comprehend.

Neurotic and reactive depression

Some psychiatrists consider that neurotic and reactive depression are the same thing; others differentiate between them. The victim of neurotic depression is said to be depressed because of a neurotic and abnormal adjustment to life, while the sufferer from a reactive depression is said to be depressed because of abnormal circumstances in life. For example, someone who experienced chronic anxiety and became depressed would be considered as suffering from neurotic depression, while a deserted wife with several children, no money and the threat of eviction might develop a reactive depression. There is little significant difference between these types of depression except for the circumstances in which they occur; one description thus suffices for both. Both are different from severe or psychotic depression, and I will examine these differences later. There is some debate as to whether psychotic depression is completely different to neurotic or reactive depression; many believe that the difference is simply one of degree. Social factors certainly play a part in the origins of severe depression. All the same there are differences in treatment between the two conditions. Neurotic and reactive depression tend to be treated by a combination of psychotherapy and social manipulation, and with reactive depression it is important to remove the environmental cause, while the treatment of severe or psychotic depression leans heavily on antidepressants and electroconvulsive therapy.

Differentiation between neurotic or reactive depression and psychotic or severe depression is usually based on symptoms and causes. In non-psychotic depression, the patient tends to have difficulty getting to sleep but does not have the problem of waking in the early morning as do most psychotically depressed people. Variation of mood through the day tends to reverse the typical pattern for psychotic depression: non-psychotic depressives feel better in the morning and deteriorate as the day goes on. Appetite is rarely affected, whereas the psychotic depressive often loses the desire to eat to a marked degree, as already seen. Neurotic and reactive depression can usually be alleviated a little by amusing company; attempts to cheer up the psychotically depressed are usually futile and sometimes make them feel worse. Thus the conditions look quite dissimilar in terms of symptom patterns. However, successful diagnosis depends largely on a careful exploration of the history of the circumstances leading up to the illness. This will expose obvious causes and allow an estimate of the degree of stress to which the patient has been subjected. Any life-long neurotic traits will generally come to light too; if they are absent, the psychiatrist may begin to suspect that the patient has endogenous depression, thus narrowing down the possibilities even further.

Regrettably, the words 'neurosis' and 'neurotic' are indis-
criminately used by many people as descriptions of character
weakness: they seem to suggest that the problem could be
solved by the patient's 'getting a grip on himself'. But neurotic
depressions are not simply invented, and people who suffer
from them are no more blameworthy than those with, for
instance, hare lips or leukaemia. All the different forms of
depression create untold misery; all depressed patients need
the right kinds of help. Most of them will have already tried
to pull themselves together, and failed.

Anxiety
Everyone has suffered anxiety at some time; it is a common,
quite normal emotion. Most people would find it difficult to
list the symptoms, but psychiatrists have to do this in order to
recognize the differences in degree and quality that divide
normal anxiety from its abnormal manifestations. All anxiety
is allied to the sensation of fear, but differs from it in quality.
Some people will say that anxiety feels like shakiness inside;
others that it is like a sense of impending death. But the
condition does have some more easily recognizable symptoms
that usually accompany the different subjective experiences
in most people's cases. The heart may beat faster than normal.
Patients may become continually aware of their breathing,
which may also be faster than usual. Their mouths may
become dry; hands may perspire; there may be a tight feeling
in the chest, or around the heart. Patients may have a sinking
feeling in the abdomen and want to go to the lavatory more
frequently than usual. Muscular weakness may occur; muscles
may tremble. The symptoms may be more severe in acute
anxiety states or panic attacks, but the more chronic anxiety
states may include any combination of these symptoms and
may last over long periods.

It can be seen from this description that anxious patients
can easily mistake their symptoms for those of physical illness,
particularly when they occur without the patient being
conscious of any special reason for anxiety. This condition
is called an anxiety neurosis when the anxiety persists over a
long period. Anxious patients may believe they have something wrong with their hearts or stomachs, or suspect they

have brain tumours. People with anxiety neurosis run the risk of developing some form of hypochondriasis.

Hypochondriasis is an abnormal concern with physical health, often to the extent that the sufferer will believe he has contracted a serious illness. If this concern is recurrent, one is likely to be told, even by some psychiatrists, that the problem is 'all in the imagination'. This is incorrect and unfair. The physical symptoms of anxiety neurosis are very real indeed. They are in themselves bewildering, and it is quite wrong that people should be told that they are imagining their illness simply because they misinterpret their symptoms. This happens in physical illness too: a person suffering from heart disease may mistakenly believe that she has a lung disorder because she is short of breath, whereas her symptoms have a quite different origin.

Anxiety may be associated with other mental illnesses, including the major psychoses. Many psychiatrists accept that it can occur alone, while others consider that when it does not seem to be associated with any other condition, it is invariably linked with some degree of depression. This distinction can be significant when treatment is being considered.

When we talk about anxiety and anxiety neurosis we must remember that anxiety is a normal experience, even sometimes useful in that it prompts us to make quick and purposeful decisions. Anxiety is only abnormal when it does not serve this useful purpose or when it is without apparent cause. The absence of obvious causes can generate further anxiety, adding fuel to an already unpleasant fire. Normal anxiety can keep us alive − abnormal anxiety can make us wish we were dead.

Phobias
An individual is suffering from a phobia when he or she becomes anxious and afraid in the presence of an object or situation that does not normally provoke anxiety.

The symptom of phobia is thus acute anxiety on exposure to a significant object or situation. Some people become panic-stricken when they are in confined spaces (claustrophobia) or wide open spaces (agoraphobia). Other people experience panic in the presence of certain animals, such as mice, snakes or cats. There is a whole range of common but lesser-known phobias, thunder phobia for instance, and in theory we can become phobic to almost anything.

Phobias are extremely common; it is likely that most of us have a mild phobia about something. Most people keep their phobias to themselves; even if they are unable to do so, they rarely seek treatment unless the phobia has a crippling effect on their lives. This happens quite often, in fact; agoraphobia keeps large numbers of people more or less permanently housebound.

Phobias can cause considerable misery, and their victims often fail to seek help because they fear they may be branded as insane or laughed at. In fact most phobias can be successfully treated; behaviourist techniques are particularly helpful, as we shall see in chapter 4.

Obsessional compulsive states

Obsessional rituals and thoughts are something we have all experienced. In childhood it is normal to practise obsessional rituals: children walk along deliberately avoiding the cracks in the pavement, touching railings in a certain calculated order, or performing other forms of ritualistic behaviour. If you ask them why, they will probably say it is a game. Quite often, however, they will say that something unpleasant will happen if they do not. Obsessional rituals have a strong flavour of magic.

In adulthood, variations on these childhood customs are commonplace. Many people like to live in a meticulously tidy way with everything in its place, a desire that is allied to obsessional behaviour and thinking. People with such tendencies tend to be inflexible in their attitudes and values, follow rules and laws carefully, and carry out their work hyper-conscientiously. However, many people with so-called obsessional personalities have difficulty in thinking independently, and few make major contributions to change, whether positive or negative. Their horizons tend to be moderate, and their thinking is sometimes restricted to the maintenance of order and the status quo.

Having an obsessional type of personality does not make a person abnormal. Only when his or her mind generates thoughts and behaviour that are unwelcome to the obsessional person and a hindrance to others does one classify the state as abnormal. The range of obsessional behaviour and thought is so great that it would be pointless to attempt to describe all the possible variations; instead I shall give some common examples to indicate what is meant by obsessional rituals and ruminations.

Perhaps the best-known obsessional ritual is that of washing the hands excessively. Sufferers may wash their hands dozens of times, not only after soiling them but also because they simply think that they have done so. Another common ritual is unnecessary checking – that the door is locked, the lights have been switched off, the gas is turned off – not once or twice but three, four, or twenty times. The victims realize that they have already checked and found everything in order, but still have to check again. Some people feel compelled to dress or undress in a special order, laying their clothes out in a particular way, and if they fail to follow this routine, or think they have, they have to repeat the whole process. Others may have to go through a ritual when they enter a room, perhaps taking one step forward, one step back and one step forward again. Some rituals are extremely complex, and can result in the sufferer spending most of his day carrying them out, at the expense of all other activity. Occasionally a person troubled by this condition tries to involve others in his rituals.

Obsessional ruminations can perhaps best be described as being akin to the experience we have all had, where a tune comes into the head and stays there unbidden and unwanted for a long period. The obsessional thoughts are often unpleasant and can be frightening when they offend the sufferer's values. Perhaps the most frightening variety is the thought that one is going to kill somebody, perhaps a child. Sometimes the thought might be that the sufferer is going to kill herself or act in some other way completely alien to her character. The ruminations may take on the form of a mathematical game: people might have to count the windows in every building they pass, and then conjure mathematically with the number in several different ways.

People who suffer from obsessional neurotic symptoms often believe they are going mad, because they realize their actions are strange and their thoughts abnormal. They can be extremely troubled, particularly when their thoughts are unpleasant ones about murder or suicide. One might expect that sufferers could stop themselves doing such things or thinking such thoughts of their own accord, but this is not so. Failure to carry out a ritual results in an overpowering attack of anxiety which forces the person back into completing it; attempts to control thoughts are equally unsuccessful. The victims of this condition often become very depressed, a state worsened by the fact that they are loath to describe their symptoms to a doctor or anyone else for fear of being laughed at or considered mad.

It must be emphasized that it is extremely rare for someone with distressing ruminations about murder or suicide ever to act on their thoughts, to do this would often be totally contrary to the principles and character of the sufferer. Nevertheless, it can happen that victims of obsessional ruminations about suicide will, in a final crisis of despair, attempt to take their own lives; in the case of ruminations about murder, however, victims will virtually never act out their thoughts.

People afflicted by obsessional compulsive states can be helped successfully. Sometimes people suffering from schizophrenia carry out obsessional rituals or make obsessionally repetitive statements, but this means only that schizophrenics can show obsessional symptoms, not that such symptoms indicate schizophrenia.

Hysteria
The concept 'hysteria' presents considerable difficulties to most psychiatrists. Many deny that the condition exists and consider that those patients who are called hysterics are in fact malingerers. This is an important subject, but before elaborating on the debate I should try to describe what is meant by hysteria, if it in fact exists.

Some individuals are said to have a hysterical personality: they tend to behave in a histrionic manner, use superlatives without restraint and describe any physical or psychiatric symptom in extravagant terms. A headache is torture; sleeplessness is driving them mad; they will never recover from the shock of discovering that their purse was missing. This type of behaviour is not a manifestation of mental illness, but simply of a personality type. There are often cultural reasons behind the development of this type of personality.

Sometimes individuals are described as being hysterical when they react strongly to pain. This is an example of 'hysterical' being used critically, in a way that is both unfair and misleading. Pain is intangible, experienced within the central nervous system, and different people's sensations of pain can vary considerably. The same person can also experience pain in different ways from time to time; for example, when under stress someone may suffer an injury and not become aware of the pain until the stress has gone.

A hysterical reaction is not the same as histrionic behaviour. The diagnosis is most frequently made when the patient appears to be suffering from some psychiatric or organic illness, but no real evidence can be found for it. He may have paralysis of a limb, yet there are none of the characteristics of an organic disease, and the condition may be cured or relieved by hypnosis or other powerful means of suggestion. Hysteria can mimic almost any physical or psychiatric disease; a description of all the possible symptoms would cover most of physical medicine and psychiatry. Loss of memory (amnesia), when not associated with head injury, is almost always hysterical in origin. That which follows head injury is usually confined to forgetting events immediately before and after the injury, but hysterical amnesia usually covers a long period and involves the sufferer forgetting not only recent events but even his or her name and address, and everything else about the past.

Mild hysterical symptoms are commonplace. The onset of a headache when one faces some unpleasant task is not unusual, but more serious manifestations of a hysterical reaction are less common.

Earlier I said that some psychiatrists deny the very existence of hysteria. Before one can accept hysteria as a reaction, it is necessary to suppose that human beings have an unconscious mind in which processes take place that affect behaviour, but of which we remain unaware. There are various explanations of the origins of hysteria, ranging from unconscious psychological conflict to faulty learning. Some people claim that hysterical reactions grow out of childhood experience, where a child has been unable to get the attention he needed from his parents and has consequently felt disregarded. Because of this he has then developed and used strategies to seek attention; these have been partially successful, and in later life he continues to use illness unconsciously as a method of gaining or trying to gain love and attention. It follows that hysterical symptoms that appear to be methods of gaining attention can be viewed as 'put on' and hence as malingering. Malingering is, of course, the deliberate mimicking of a disease to achieve some advantage, such as compensation, exemption from unpleasant duties, or a way into a more comfortable situation. Servicemen may malinger to get themselves excused fatigues, or a prisoner may malinger in order to enjoy the relative ease of the prison hospital.

Other doctors object to the diagnosis of hysteria for other, and perhaps better, reasons. A disturbing number of patients initially diagnosed as suffering from hysteria have been found on further investigation to be suffering from an organic disease which presented itself in an unusual way. A well-known psychiatrist has said that when physicians talk of hysteria you should send for the undertaker. One young man, treated by hypnosis for nine months for the recurrent paralysis of his arm, finally died from a small semi-mobile tumour of the brain found near the upper part of his spinal cord.

A reasonable assessment might be as follows: there are malingerers, and to deny their existence would be foolish. Most malingerers in everyday life have some emotional problems which cause their malingering, and they need positive help rather than abuse. Genuinely hysterical symptoms can and do occur, but they may be associated with some other underlying illness, either physical or mental. It is dangerous to attach the label of hysteria to anybody until it is quite clear that there is no underlying illness. Doctors regularly claim that 'fashions' in hysteria vary, using this as an argument in favour of classifying all hysterical symptoms as special forms of malingering. This is not a convincing argument, since 'fashions' in organic diseases are also recognized.

Anorexia nervosa

This condition, which is not uncommon, causes the sufferers to lose all desire to eat so that they regard most food, particularly that of any nutritional value, with revulsion. They stop eating, though continue to drink; lose weight dramatically; and will die if untreated. Even though they are not eating, they may live active lives until they either accept treatment or succumb.

Anorexia nervosa usually occurs in girls and women between the ages of fourteen and thirty, but occasionally affects young men. It sometimes begins when the patient is dieting to lose weight, but there is often some hidden emotional conflict involved; for example, a girl suffering from the condition may be engaged and have serious doubts about her future.

The condition is quite serious and usually requires inpatient treatment, consisting of sympathetic encouragement to eat, preferably by one nurse with whom the patient may develop a rapport. In parallel with this practical method of treatment it is essential that psychological investigation is also carried out to expose and deal with the underlying emotional problem. Treatment properly administered is almost invariably successful. Behavioural methods of treatment are also effective; here the patient is rewarded for putting on weight.

Personality disorders

It has already been mentioned that some psychiatrists would use the term personality disorder to encompass all mental abnormalities that are not psychotic. This has many disadvantages, and it may be better to confine the term to those people who have certain facets of personality that are an exaggeration of the normal range. Some people are trusting, while others tend to be suspicious of others; this is an example of the normal range of attitudes. However, if someone's suspiciousness is extreme she may be thought to have a 'paranoid' personality and hence a personality disorder. There is a great number of personality traits and each one can be present to an abnormal degree. Most psychiatrists consider that personality disorders are untreatable, though psychoanalysts tend not to agree.

Further confusion arises when the term personality disorder is used as a synonym for psychopathy, itself sometimes a misleading term. Before discussing the concept of psychopathy I should emphasize that people with personality disorders in the narrower sense are simply people with exaggerated personality traits. Some of these may cause an individual difficulties and affect his or her relationship with others and with the wider society; other types of personality disorder harm no one.

Psychopathy

Psychopathy and psychopath are terms that tend to be used frequently and loosely. The very words have confusion built into them: the literal meaning of psychopathy is 'abnormality of the psyche', so the term could logically be applied to any victim of mental illness. However, it is not used in this way but confined to individuals who have certain socially unacceptable characteristics.

The psychopath, as understood by psychiatry, is someone whose most prominent characteristic is unreliability. He will lie, cheat, let you down and yet return time and time again expecting to be believed and trusted. He never learns from experience and underestimates other people's intelligence. Many psychiatrists consider that the basic problem of the psychopath is that he is unable to relate to other people. He tends to lack the ability to be sensitive to other people's feelings and to respond appropriately. This failure is believed to be caused by a number of possible factors, including separation from the mother or father at a critical period in development and certain forms of brain damage or immaturity of the brain.

In the Mental Health Act of 1959, psychopathic disorder is defined as

> a persistent disorder, or disability of mind (whether or not including subnormality of intelligence), which results in abnormally aggressive, or seriously irresponsible conduct on the part of the patient, and requires or is susceptible to medical treatment.

The Mental Health (Amendment) Bill suggests that this definition should be changed to a persistent disorder, or disability of mind (whether or not including significant impairment of intelligence), which results in abnormally aggressive, or seriously irresponsible conduct on the part of the patient.

The Bill thus omits the mention of medical treatment, a step in keeping with the views of the many psychiatrists who consider that psychopathy is untreatable.

Different types of psychopath have been identified: the inadequate psychopath, simply unable to deal with the normal problems of life; the aggressive psychopath, liable to become violent on the slightest provocation, or simply because it gives him pleasure, the hysterical psychopath, who exhibits some of the minor symptoms of hysteria and constantly demands attention; and the creative psychopath, who may produce works of art or achieve considerable fame in some creative field, but who otherwise behaves in a remarkably irresponsible, anti-social way.

Almost all of us behave a little like this at some time, so that in a sense psychopathy can be seen as a specific, severe form of personality disorder, although classifying it as such is not very comforting to people who have personality disorders of a non-psychopathic nature. The behaviour of some psychopathic people is less offensive than that of others, but since the word does suggest 'badness' of some kind to most people, it is best to reserve the label for those who do actually harm others. Whether psychopaths should be considered 'bad' or 'sick' is debatable, but on the whole the notion of sickness or abnormality is more appropriate, since the condition does have certain easily recognizable features and can be traced back to possible causes. The effect of childhood experience in forming the psychopathic personality may still be in the realm of speculation, but there is hard evidence to demonstrate that brain damage can bring about psychopathic behaviour.

It should also be remembered that some people who enjoy great success in our society exhibit all the characteristics of the so-called psychopath, only differing from their fellow sufferers — who may end up in prison — by being more intelligent or more skilled at manipulation. No profession or occupation is free of individuals with this type of personality.

The orthodox view on psychopathy is that it is untreatable; on the other hand, there is evidence to suggest that most psychopaths can in fact be helped. Most improve as they grow older even without treatment, provided they are not harmed by society's reaction to their behaviour. Long periods of imprisonment or incarceration in psychiatric institutions do not help in themselves but are unfortunately sometimes necessary for the protection of other people.

Sexual abnormalities

It is extremely difficult to define normal sexual behaviour: there are many types of sexual activity, and some that have been viewed as abnormal in the past are now accepted as completely normal. For example, masturbation is practised by the majority of people, both men and women, at some time. Yet many people, including professionals, still describe it as abnormal behaviour and conjure up imaginary ill effects said to arise from it. The view of masturbation prevalent in society can turn this innocent behaviour into a problem; when we consider sexual abnormality it is important to remember that the behaviour itself may often be statistically normal and quite innocuous, but because of social attitudes the individual may suffer much anxiety and guilt and so become abnormally distressed in psychological terms.

One definition popular some years ago was that any sexual act that did not lead to normal sexual intercourse between a male and female was a perversion. This rigid definition would even make kissing a perversion if it was not the prelude to sexual intercourse. Now we tend to use two criteria for deciding if a form of sexual activity constitutes illness: if it engenders anxiety or guilt in the person concerned, or if it is dangerous or damaging to that person or to anyone else. So, for example, a male homosexual who fully accepted his desires and behaviour and involved himself only with other homosexuals of a similar outlook would not be considered ill. But another man who had strong homosexual feelings and regarded them as sinful and himself as abnormal, or even sick, would be in need of help, and it would be reasonable to classify his emotional state as illness.

There is such a range of sexual activity that to explore it

in any detail would turn this section into a volume. Here I shall discuss only the more common sexual abnormalities and the emotional problems that accompany them.

Impotence, premature ejaculation and frigidity are problems that affect large numbers of people. Impotence usually means a physical failure on the part of the male to carry out the sex act. It is usually due to difficulty in producing or maintaining a satisfactory erection of the penis, and can occur every time intercourse is attempted or only with particular partners or on particular occasions. Premature ejaculation is a condition where the male ejaculates very early in the sexual act, usually before penetration. Frigidity is a term applied only to women and covers a range of problems, from finding sexual intercourse repugnant to passively accepting intercourse but experiencing no pleasure and failing to reach a climax. All these problems can be short-lived or can continue over a long period. There are many causes, ranging from loss of interest in the sexual partner to more deep-seated anxieties. Often an episode of impotence or anxiety about intercourse can have a direct and short-lived cause, but then this experience can itself engender deep-rooted anxieties that perpetuate the condition even though the original cause is no longer present. Competent professional help is essential; often sexual abnormalities result from sheer ignorance as well as the causes I have already mentioned.

Paedophilia (sexual activity with children) is a serious and not uncommon problem. Some societies permit sexual activity in relatively young children, but in ours it is taboo; anyone who does attempt some form of sexual relationship with a child is thus likely to be called abnormal. The law invariably regards such people as criminals, perhaps unfairly, since they are inevitably victims of abnormal sexual drives that are extremely difficult to resist. Most people with normal heterosexual leanings are not forced always to deny their sexual urges, and the people who do are often those with a low level of sexual interest.

Incest is also taboo and illegal in our society but occurs more frequently than many people realize. It is difficult to know how to evaluate incest where illness is concerned. A recent investigation suggested that it is not so abnormal as many people think, and some of the cases examined revealed little evidence of harm to those involved.

The last two sexual deviations that I shall discuss always cause considerable public anxiety. Exhibitionism, when the individual, usually male, exposes his sex organs to a female, casually and often in a public place, is quite common and provokes much anger. Many women have had a man expose himself to them in this way at some time or other. The exhibitionist is usually a shy, withdrawn man, that is to say, he is suffering from a personality disorder; he is riddled with sexual inhibitions, but completely harmless. Exhibitionists may expose themselves but they are not likely to do anything else. They should receive our sympathy and nothing else, for they are in need of help. They certainly do not deserve the anger and disgust that they usually meet.

Sado-masochism is quite a different order of problem. Sadism means obtaining sexual pleasure from hurting someone; masochism is obtaining that pleasure from being hurt oneself. Sadists can thus be dangerous to others, masochists to themselves. Both can be helped, though extreme sadists have to be confined to protect people from their violence. They can quite properly be considered as psychopaths. Whilst it is important to remember that some small degree of sado-masochism is displayed by many people, here we are discussing the extremes, when sadists can kill, and masochists can seek such an intensity of pain that they may die in realizing it.

Our society is still quite inhibited in sexual matters, despite popular statements to the contrary. A remarkable number of people continue to regard sex as dirty. This distorted and irrational view of something which is, in itself, clearly normal and innocent affects us all, but some people more acutely than others. An unhealthy attitude in society makes some of its members sick in turn; society then responds with anger and punishment. It would be rational to try to cure the problem by changing social attitudes, but this would require immense effort and so, for the time being, we have to concentrate on helping the people who are harmed by society's outlook. It is important to bear in mind society's attitude towards sex; people can be oppressed by distorted ideas about normal sexual practices or by the guilt that often springs from religious teachings and children's folk lore. A vital step to improving this sorry state of affairs is to make more information about sex and sexuality available to everyone.

The treatment of sexual offenders presents considerable difficulties since their response to psychotherapy is not particularly encouraging. Drugs that reduce the sex drive have sometimes been administered, but since they affect people quite dramatically and can produce unpleasant side-effects there are strong arguments against their use. There is also a moral problem: it can be argued that prisoners are not in a position to give free consent to such treatment since they are under pressure to conform in prison and may also be offered incentives such as early parole if they accept the drugs. People might accept hormone or other drug treatment for their sexual abnormality while they are in prison, even though they would reject it completely if they were free citizens.

Addictions

Most people think that addiction means drug addiction, something to do with opium, heroin, morphine, pep pills, mescaline and LSD. The Victorians talked about 'drug fiends', and the picture this term conjures up is still alive today. People tend to think of drug addicts as depraved, dangerous and sinister — a far from accurate image.

In medicine and psychiatry it is common to talk about two types of addiction: physical and psychological. It used to be thought that certain drugs, taken over a period of time, created a physical dependence. But to draw sharp borders between physical and psychological addiction is mistaken, for the information available is confusing and does not entirely support a differentiation. It seems more reasonable to say simply that a patient is addicted to a drug whenever he or she is dependent on it to carry on normal life. The present tendency is in fact to talk of drug dependence.

The major drugs used by members of our society that involve addiction or dependence are tobacco, alcohol and the barbiturates rather than heroin, marijuana, LSD and the opiates. The barbiturates are a group of drugs still commonly used as sedatives and include sodium amytal and the mixture of two barbiturates marketed in the United Kingdom as Tuinal. Another well known barbiturate, phenobarbitone, is still used in the treatment of epilepsy and occasionally as a sedative. Tobacco, alcohol and the barbiturates cause more illness, misery and instability than any other addictive drugs.

Tobacco   Most people who smoke are addicted to tobacco, find it very difficult or even impossible to give it up, and suffer ill effects for a period afterwards if they succeed. The ill effects of tobacco are now well established. Not only does cigarette smoking play an important part in the creation of lung cancer, but it has also been identified as a cause of heart and arterial disease and various chest ailments. If there is anything rational in the prohibition of drugs, tobacco qualifies without reservation.

Alcohol   Drinking alcohol moderately is not harmful; indeed, in many ways it seems to be beneficial. Unfortunately, some people develop a real addiction to alcohol. They drink excessively, either regularly or in bouts, and their whole existence revolves around the bottle. Every facet of life is affected, so that they may find it difficult to keep a job, and relationships with their families may deteriorate. Health can be seriously affected, not only because of the direct effect of alcohol but because alcoholics tend not to eat when drinking heavily and suffer as a result from nutrient deficiencies, particularly deficiencies of the B-complex vitamins. Permanent damage to the liver may occur, and there can even be irreversible brain damage.

Alcoholics, like all those who become dependent on a drug, even, perhaps, those addicted to tobacco, suffer from some underlying psychological problem and perhaps a degree of personality abnormality. Alcoholism can be a dreadful affliction; in severe cases hallucinations and delirium tremens (DTs) can occur, though not every alcoholic is affected in this way. Alcoholics can and do respond well to treatment, but we are still only scratching at the surface of the problem, which is grave both for patients and for their family and friends.

Barbiturates There are large numbers of barbiturate addicts, particularly among middle-aged women. Doctors must take some responsibility for this problem. Huge quantities of barbiturates are prescribed every year, in spite of both the availability of other, less dangerous, sedatives and repeated appeals to doctors not to prescribe sedatives of any kind unless there are compelling reasons for doing so. There is still a place for phenobarbitone in the treatment of epilepsy, and certain quick-acting barbiturates are needed in anaesthesia. These are the only legitimate uses for barbiturates, and they should have no secondary function as sedatives.

Barbiturates can produce a pleasant, hazy, drunken-seeming euphoria, and it is this quality that gains them so many victims. Once someone has become dependent it can be extremely difficult and, unless done with great care, danger-ous to wean them off the drugs. It has been said that if a barbiturate addict and a heroin addict were locked away in separate rooms without access to drugs and left for three days, the chances are that the heroin addict would survive and the barbiturate addict die. Among other effects, the sudden withdrawal of barbiturates can produce epileptic-type fits which may, if not treated, become continuous and result in death.

The opiates and other 'hard' drugs This category includes heroin, morphine, pethidine and similar drugs. Opiates can rapidly cause addiction in susceptible subjects. Probably most people are not susceptible and would not become addicted, but this does not mean that the opiates are harmless and should be accessible to everyone since it is impossible to anticipate who might be prone to addiction; once it sets in it may be too late to act.

It is difficult accurately to assess the effects of opiate addiction because so many factors complicate the picture. Addicts may be social outcasts; they often participate in criminal activities to secure their drugs; and the substances they obtain may contain numerous impurities. Under such conditions the life of an untreated addict is limited and miserable. His whole existence centres on the drug, and he lives from one dose or 'fix' to the next. In the past opium used to be smoked; now opiates are taken by injection, either under the skin, into a muscle or directly into the blood stream ('mainlining'). This method carries serious dangers in itself; the equipment used is often dirty and can place addicts at the risk of contracting infections such as blood poisoning (septicaemia) and infection of the liver (viral hepatitis), both of which can be fatal.

Like all addicts, people dependent upon opiates can be treated and helped, but at present more money and effort are invested in police activity connected with addicts than in humane treatment. Addicts are harassed, hunted and punished. Ironically, many of those responsible for this oppression are themselves addicted to tobacco, and some to alcohol.

Amphetamines   There are a number of different amphetamines or pep pills, all members of the same group. Dexamphetamine, or Dexedrine, and methylamphetamine, or Methedrine, are possibly the best known. Drinamyl, or purple hearts, was once extensively used but has now been removed from the market. It was a mixture of amphetamine and a barbiturate, making it a doubly dangerous preparation. Amphetamines are stimulants, increasing activity and counteracting sleep. They often produce a feeling of euphoria, but not always; some people find their effect rather unpleasant. At one time amphetamines were prescribed for depression, but now most doctors refuse to use them under any conditions, in contrast to the common practice of prescribing dangerous barbiturates. Perhaps one reason is that most abusers of amphetamines are young people, while those of barbiturates are usually middle-aged.

Small doses of amphetamines are not particularly harmful, but once someone has tried them there is always the danger that they will take more. Some amphetamine users consume extraordinarily large amounts; such doses may have a severe impact on behaviour, ranging from complete irresponsibility to a state of confusion in which the sufferer may be unaware of his or her surroundings and behave in a bizarre and sometimes dangerous manner. Overdosage of amphetamines can produce a disorder similar to schizophrenia.

Mescaline and LSD These drugs are not addictive and there are no withdrawal symptoms when they are stopped. To varying degrees they produce disturbances of consciousness during which hallucinations are experienced. Distortions of time occur, and the user escapes into an unreal world that may be fascinating and pleasant or frightening and disturbing (a 'bad trip'). There is some evidence that susceptible people may become psychotic as a result of taking these drugs. The findings are somewhat contradictory, but there are indications that someone with the appropriate predisposition can be pushed into actual schizophrenia if he or she takes these drugs.

LSD used occasionally to be used in the treatment of the neuroses in the attempt to help patients gain insight into their problems. Most of the people whom I have seen treated with LSD have described it as a disorientating and distressing experience.

Cannabis, hashish or 'pot' Large numbers of young people regularly smoke cannabis, so that it is now becoming a statistically normal practice. Leaving aside the question of whether the smoking of cannabis should be legalized, it seems that it has little if any ill effect on the user, is possibly less harmful than tobacco and does not promote disturbed behaviour. It may be that in the future cannabis will supplant tobacco as the accepted addiction, though tobacco is commonly mixed with cannabis when it is smoked.

Withdrawal symptoms and addiction

Certain addictive drugs, particularly opiates, produce unpleasant physical withdrawal symptoms when someone who takes them regularly ceases to do so. These symptoms include abdominal and muscle cramps, headache, vomiting, salivation and excessive secretion from the nose and eyes. Whether withdrawal symptoms have a physical or psychological basis is a matter of debate. Ill effects of many different kinds can follow the withdrawal of drugs from people who have come to rely on them excessively; acute anxiety might be an example. Some people are more prone to addiction than others, but most are in no danger of becoming addicted to anything, even when taking drugs over a long period of time for medical reasons. At the other extreme are those unfortunates who seem capable of becoming addicted to almost any substance. Because of some underlying psychological abnormality or disturbance, certain people are liable to become addicted to something even after a casual encounter with it; happily, though, this is an exceptional state of affairs.

The most important factor in the treatment of addiction is the motivation of the addict. It is impossible to treat successfully an addict who does not want to be helped. Of course, addicts can be kept in confinement so that they cannot obtain drugs, but this form of cure can only last while restraint continues. This being so, perhaps we should allow addicts who are not motivated towards cure to continue their addiction without official harassment, for they do little harm to anyone but themselves, unless it is to people who are fond of them, or to other vulnerable people if they also act as 'drug-pushers'.

Organic brain disease

It is customary to consider this subject under two main headings.

Acute toxic confusional state
Most people experience this condition at some time in their lives, probably in childhood, when delirium occurs as a result of an acute infection, chemical intoxication, or other serious disturbance of the body metabolism. Adults are much less prone to this experience than children, though its frequency increases with advancing age. Depending on whether the cause is an infection, some patients will run unusually high temperatures.

The psychological symptoms of acute toxic confusion include some loss of contact with the environment. This can vary intermittently – the patient can be relatively aware for some time and then lose touch again quite quickly. Patients are restless and may experience hallucinations. Any area of the senses may be affected; some people experience a disturbed sense of touch, feeling things as rougher or smoother than they actually are; others are affected visually, so that what they see may be grossly distorted, the room becoming larger or smaller than it really is, with walls leaning inwards or out- wards; others may pick at the bedclothes, call out to imaginary people, or become terrified and aggressive by turns. A con- dition called occupational delirium may also occur, in which the patient behaves as if he were at work.

There are many causes of acute toxic confusion, all producing some disturbance of the body chemistry. The treatment of this condition consists of the treatment of the underlying cause. There is no evidence that acute toxic con- fusion indicates the presence of any psychological problems in the sufferer. People of a stable disposition can develop this condition if they succumb to certain illnesses or are given certain drugs.

Dementia

The word dementia can be misleading, since it is often used to describe an individual's behaviour. In fact dementia denotes the result of chronic irreversible brain damage and should never be applied loosely to other conditions.

The symptoms of dementia include disturbances of memory, particularly of the recent past; loss of reasoning ability; disorientation in time and place so that the patient may be unsure of the date or time of year or where he is; and extreme emotional variability so that sufferers will laugh or cry for little reason, fluctuating between extremes in rapid succession.

The causes of dementia are the same conditions that pro- duce brain damage. The following list is not comprehensive but suggests the range of possible factors: infections that attack brain tissue, such as syphilis; long-standing vitamin deficiencies, particularly of the B-complex; deficiencies of certain hormones; tumours; interference with the blood supply to the brain; and serious head injuries.

There is also a group of conditions that produce brain damage by decreasing the number of brain cells; their origins are not clearly understood but they are recognizable as diseases, though unfortunately they are still usually called dementias of one kind or another. The best known of these are the so-called pre-senile dementias and the senile dementia that occurs in extreme old age. Pre-senile dementia, as the term implies, is similar to that of old age but attacks a much younger age group. Older people who develop dementia usually suffer either from this so-called senile dementia or from interference with the blood supply to the brain due to blood vessel degeneration, normally known as arteriosclerotic dementia. One type of pre-senile dementia is called Alzheimer's disease. Where it is present specific changes can be found in the brain, and similar changes occur in senile dementia. It is now considered that senile dementia is possibly a form of Alzheimer's disease. This is a step forward, but our understanding of the cause of this condition is still very limited.

Mental illness in all its guises causes much individual misery and some anxiety to society in general. However, much can be done to help, and in the next chapter I shall examine the forms of treatment and services available.

4 Facilities, Services and Treatment

In the past, facilities for treating mental illness were limited mainly to institutional care. A few hospitals, located mainly in London and other major cities, did provide a limited out-patient service, but it was not accessible to the majority of people in this country. There were limited private facilities, but again there tended to be an emphasis on treatment and care within an institution. Since the Second World War there have been dramatic changes in our concepts of mental illness and its treatment. It is important to bear in mind that one in ten of the population will come under treatment at some time or another for mental illness.

Most people who develop psychiatric disorders can and should be treated in the community, and facilities are continually being developed to make this possible. A few individuals seem to need treatment within an institutional setting, but the chief reason for placing someone in an institution is rather to protect the public than actually to help the individual. Official services can be considered under three main headings; the family doctor, the hospital, and local authority services. Naturally these services are interdependent and should run closely in parallel; close cooperation between them is vital if mentally ill people are truly to be helped.

Facilities and services

Family doctors

The family doctor can be described as the front line in the treatment of mental illness. The great majority of people who are troubled with an emotional problem or develop a mental illness seek help first from their family doctors. Doctors treat most of the patients they see without referring them to the specialist psychiatric services. When they do refer patients for psychiatric opinion, they often administer the treatment with the help of the specialist. Patients who have been admitted to psychiatric hospitals return to their family doctors after discharge. The treatment they provide is rarely in isolation, since they will be assisted by other health service workers — such as health visitors and nurses — and local authority workers — such as social workers, home helps, and so on. The role of the family doctor is an extremely important one, since he or she is usually the one professional who knows the patient's family background and is closely in touch with the community to which he or she belongs. It is also the family doctor who decides if specialist help is required and what kind should be sought. When a patient needs to be admitted to hospital, it is usually the family doctor who makes the appropriate arrangements, and if admission is thought to be possible only under a compulsory order, it is again generally the family doctor who initiates the process. If a court requires medical evidence about a patient, the family doctor is often in a position to give the most useful information.

The hospital service

The hospital service provides special facilities for the mentally ill. Each district has a psychiatric hospital and/or a general hospital psychiatric unit. Psychiatrists are available to see patients in their own homes, in outpatient clinics, or in hospitals. The precise nature of provision in the hospital psychiatric services varies considerably from district to district, and it is important to find out what is available in your own district and whether it is possible to use facilities in other areas if they are not available locally. Every district has inpatient, outpatient and domiciliary services, but there may also be specialist units for neurosis, alcoholism, drug dependency, adolescents, the elderly and people with personality disorders. There is always special provision for children, but it is often limited to outpatient facilities. Similarly, there will always be some treatment available to adolescents, but there may not be an adolescent inpatient unit in the local district.

Since the current emphasis falls on treating patients in the community, the hospital service no longer limits its activities to the various institutions but also provides direct help within the home. This ranges from domiciliary consultations with psychiatrists to the provision of community psychiatric nurses, the involvement of social workers and intervention in times of crisis. Some districts have emergency teams consisting of doctors, social workers and nurses who are able to go out to patients in trouble or distress and provide the necessary help in the home.

In this country, services for the mentally ill tend to be distinct from services for the mentally handicapped, though there is considerable overlap. Most districts will have a psychiatric service and a separate mental handicap service; both will provide the range of facilities I have mentioned, though on the whole services for the mentally handicapped tend to be less adequate than those for the mentally ill.

Local authority services
The 1974 reorganization of the Health Service and of local government has wrought significant changes in local authority provision. In the past, each local authority had a health department, with a medical officer of health, district nurses, health visitors and other workers involved in community medicine and services. Medical officers of health have now become community physicians and work in the Health Service; district nurses and health visitors have also become Health Service employees. The main contribution made by local authorities at present is by way of their social services departments. These provide social workers who work mainly in the community but also have hospital commitments, and a variety of domiciliary services, including home helps, meals-on-wheels and laundry provision. The social services department is also responsible for day centres for the mentally ill, training centres for the mentally handicapped, day nurseries, old people's homes, hostels and homes for the mentally disordered and mentally handicapped, and children's homes. They also operate fostering and boarding-out schemes for children and mentally ill and mentally handicapped people.

The local authority is further involved by way of its education and housing departments. The education department provides special schools for mentally handicapped children, day nursery schools, remedial teachers, educational welfare officers and educational psychologists. The housing department is involved in the provision of special housing, particularly for the elderly and physically handicapped.

Voluntary organizations

A number of voluntary organizations provide services and help for the mentally ill and mentally handicapped, ranging from day centres and clubs to hostels, group homes, active treatment facilities in some places, and crisis intervention services. It is not possible to give full details here about voluntary organizations and their facilities, since these vary so much from one district to another, but it is important to discover what is available in your own district if you are seeking help or advice, or making decisions about someone who is mentally ill. It is surprising how often people are treated in a particular way not because it is chosen as the best or most appropriate method but because of ignorance as to what other options are available.

Special facilities for the mentally ill offender

All the services described are available for mentally ill offenders. Those awaiting trial can be referred to psychiatric outpatient departments if necessary; this is always the best way of obtaining a psychiatric opinion. But if the offender must for some reason be kept in prison, a psychiatrist can visit the prison to give an opinion. Sometimes the need for a medical opinion appears to be the only reason for remanding people in custody; this is quite inappropriate, since it is easier to obtain an opinion by referring people to an outpatient department than it is to ask a psychiatrist to visit the prison. The assessment can be far more satisfactorily carried out in an outpatient department, since special tests and investigations can then follow. It is also rather unfair on the accused to commit him or her to prison simply because a psychiatric opinion is required.

Once it has been decided that someone is mentally ill and guilty of an offence, it is possible for him or her to receive treatment within the normal psychiatric facilities of the district. This may consist of outpatient or inpatient treatment, carried out informally, as a condition of probation, or under compulsion. Unfortunately the staff of some psychiatric hospitals are loath to treat offenders as inpatients, and this presents difficulties which I shall discuss in greater detail in chapter 13. It is important to discover whether a psychiatric service will admit an offender, though, since resistance is not universal and depends upon the mental illness from which the offender is suffering and the crime he or she has committed.

The special hospitals
Some mentally ill offenders may be considered so dangerous that they require treatment in secure establishments. Again I should emphasize that only a fraction of mentally ill individuals are violent or dangerous.

Section 4 of the National Health Service Act 1977 requires the Secretary of State for Social Services to maintain establishments 'for persons subject to detention under the Mental Health Act 1959 who in his opinion require treatment under conditions of special security on account of their dangerous, violent or criminal propensities'. There are at present three such special hospitals – Broadmoor in Berkshire, Rampton in Nottinghamshire, and Moss Side near Liverpool. In addition a fourth is under construction on a site adjacent to the hospital at Moss Side. The special hospitals differ from NHS psychiatric hospitals in that all of their patients are subject to detention under the Mental Health Act, and treatment is carried out inside a highly secure boundary. The security of the special hospitals is intended to deter the persistent absconder and to prevent the escape of patients who would, if free, present a grave danger to the public. The level of security is such as to make it virtually impossible to escape.

The special hospitals are administered directly by the Secretary of State – the only hospitals in England and Wales so governed. The functions of management vested in the Secretary of State, including decisions on admission, are exercised through senior officers at the hospitals and administrative and professional staff in London. The aim of the special hospitals is to provide treatment under conditions of maximum security, achieved by a high staff to patient ratio and effective information and communication systems combined with adequate physical means of security such as restricted numbers of exits and entrances, locked doors and perimeter walls. Successful treatment also contributes to security.

At present Broadmoor accommodates about 750 patients (625 male and 125 female), most of whom are suffering from mental illness or a psychopathic disorder. Rampton Hospital provides accommodation for approximately 950 patients (700 male and 250 female), most of whom suffer from mental subnormality or psychopathic disorders, although there are also some mentally ill patients. Moss Side accommodates about 375 patients (300 male and 75 female), most of whom are suffering from mental subnormality or psychopathic disorder. As in Rampton, there is a minority of patients suffering from mental illness. In general the patients accommodated at Moss Side are less dangerous than those accommodated at Broadmoor and Rampton.

The construction of the new Park Lane Hospital was begun in 1976. It is intended eventually to accommodate 410 patients suffering from mental illness there, thus alleviating the overcrowding in Broadmoor. The hospital is now partially open, with eight wards providing 200 places. It is hoped that the final four wards will be opened in 1984.

Therapeutic communities
There are a number of other units that treat mentally ill offenders throughout the country. The Henderson Hospital in Surrey is a long-established therapeutic community that specializes in the treatment of individuals suffering from psychopathic disorders. Patients can be referred to this hospital, but it cannot be forced to admit anyone. Since it functions as a community, individuals who are referred are assessed by both patients and staff, and the decision as to whether they are acceptable is taken at a meeting attended by patients.

Patients with drug dependency problems are accepted in special units, which vary both in their willingness to accept offenders and in the regimes they provide. Alpha House in Southampton is run as a therapeutic community for drug addicts or misusers. It differs from the Henderson Hospital in being hierarchically structured, with an emphasis on discipline and personal responsibility. Alpha House is run by Hampshire County Council social services department but does take individuals from other parts of the country.

The Ley Clinic at Oxford is another example of a special facility for drug offenders. Situated in the grounds of Little-more Hospital, the local psychiatric establishment, it is run on therapeutic community lines but with an emphasis again on a more structured, hierarchical society than is usually the case in therapeutic communities.

These three examples illustrate the kind of facilities that may be available, serving either a specific area or the whole country. It is not possible to describe everything that is available; new projects are continually being started, others may fail. Therefore it is important to explore carefully what is available whenever decisions are being made about an individual's future and the possibilities of treatment.

Facilities in prisons
Sadly, more and more mentally abnormal offenders are being sent to prison because no one else will accept them. Most prisons provide some sort of psychiatric treatment: some have visiting psychiatrists and psychotherapists, while others have prison medical officers who are particularly interested in and concerned about mental illness. The prison service also has a psychiatric hospital of its own, Grendon Prison at Grendon Underwood. There is considerable misunderstanding about Grendon; courts often sentence people to prison with a strong recommendation that they should be sent there, but in fact the only people empowered to refer individuals to Grendon are prison medical officers. A court may advise that an offender should go to Grendon Prison, but it should be pointed out clearly to the prisoner that this is a recommendation only, and whether he goes there depends on the opinion of the medical officer of the prison to which he will be sent, and on his being acceptable to the Grendon staff. Grendon tends to specialize in the treatment of intelligent psychopaths. It is certainly not a prison hospital for the dangerous, aggressive individual.

Treatment

The treatment of psychiatric disorders can never be restricted merely to the attentions of doctors and other professional staff. Treatment always involves interaction between the patient and the people who are trying to help, with the patient playing an active role. The prescribing of a drug, or the ordering of a course of ECT, may play a part in treatment, but if it stops there it is likely to fail. Treatment in psychiatry is not confined to encounters with doctors; it begins at the very moment the patient consults someone about his or her problem. It is concerned with the act of putting a problem into words and with the mechanics of formal diagnosis. It will continue in all kinds of ways, involving many people, and always, if it is to be successful, with the active involvement of the patient.

The milieu of treatment, the kind of community in which the patient is treated, is all-important. It should be as open as possible, combining support and help with a freedom to act independently and express problems and difficulties without fear of criticism or scorn.

Bearing this in mind, I shall give a broad outline of specific treatments; these can be most effective for treating identified problems, provided that the patient is treated as a person and encouraged to relate to others and discover his or her inner self.

Psychotherapy

Psychotherapy can mean many things, from a formal Freudian analysis to a few brief interviews with a psychiatrist. It can be carried out on an individual basis, or in groups. Formal psychoanalysis is difficult to obtain because of the relatively small number of trained analysts and its time-consuming nature. Patients may require an hour's psychotherapy every day, leaving the therapist free to see no more than seven or eight patients at any one time. A full course of psychotherapy might continue for two or more years, so it can be seen that the total number of patients one analyst can treat is severely limited. However, there are other types of psychotherapy which are less demanding of time, and, in group psychotherapy, where much larger numbers of patients can be treated.

On the whole psychotheraphy is used to treat neurotic reactions, but there are therapists who believe they can play an important part in the treatment of psychotic illnesses, such as schizophrenia and severe depression.

Occupational therapy

Occupational therapy no longer means just making baskets and rugs; it now embraces industrial therapy, social activities, household management and entertainment. The occupational therapist can play a vital part in the therapeutic team, providing occupation, entertainment and other activities that restore the patient's sense of worth and usefulness. Industrial therapy, in which tasks tailored to the ability of the patient are carried out to produce useful articles and financial remuneration, can do much to restore the individual's self-respect. Whatever activity is provided, patients usually experience greater benefit if it is performed as part of a group, since this offers the chance to improve their ability to deal with, relate to and communicate with others. Entertainment can include anything from listening to records to organizing and participating in social evenings, and can be as valuable as any other type of occupational therapy.

Behaviour therapy

Behaviour therapy is based on the original work of Pavlov, Watson and Skinner. In simple terms, it depends on conditioning and de-conditioning. Practitioners who use behaviour therapy sometimes make rather extravagant claims, but there is accumulating evidence to show that it does have a place among the forms of psychiatric treatment. It can be effective in the treatment of phobic states; many patients who were once housebound are now able to live normal lives because this technique has been successfully used to help them. There do exist unacceptable behaviourist techniques, however, which usually involve attempts to associate undesirable types of behaviour with pain, or some other unpleasant experience. Such techniques, like others such as brain-washing, are to be condemned.

Electroplexy and psychosurgery
Electroplexy, or ECT, consists of inducing an epileptic fit in the patient by passing a low current of electricity through the brain. The patient is anaesthetized and given a muscle relaxant before treatment, to minimize any convulsion. It is usual to give a course of between six and eight treatments, spaced over a period of three to four weeks. ECT is only effective in the treatment of severe depression, and the introduction of antidepressant drugs has meant that it is less popular than formerly and will probably fade away from the therapeutic scene in the next few years.

Leucotomy and other types of psychosurgery are still employed but there is a tendency now to avoid them since they are irreversible, often have little positive impact and may have a gravely harmful effect upon the patient's personality. The purpose of leucotomy is to reduce anxiety, and when it is used on some victims of severe obsessional neurosis the improvement can be dramatic. But as I have said, there is an increasing opposition to the use of these techniques, and on the whole they are not to be recommended.

There has been a great deal of concern over the treatment of compulsorily detained patients with electroplexy or psychosurgery against their wishes. The law has not been clear on this point, but the Mental Health (Amendment) Bill now recommends that compulsorily detained patients should receive certain treatments against their wishes only if an independent doctor approved by the Secretary of State has examined them and agrees that there is a need for such treatment. I shall discuss this matter later in relation to consent.

Drug therapy
The drugs used commonly in psychiatry can be divided into three main groups.

Tranquillizers   Tranquillizers are preparations that are said to counter anxiety and agitation without producing sedation. This is partly true, but most tranquillizers, if taken in sufficient amounts, also produce sedation, and in some people even relatively small doses can produce considerable sedation. Tranquillizers are conventionally divided into the major and minor varieties. The latter group includes medazepam (Nobrium) and diazepam (Valium); the major tranquillizers include chlorpromazine (Largactil), trifluoperazine (Stelazine), thioridazine (Melleril), fluphenazine (Moditen), and flupen-thixol (Depixol). The minor tranquillizers are normally used in the treatment of anxiety and agitation; the major ones are used for schizophrenia, paraphrenia and other so-called psychotic reactions. This is not to say that there is a sharp boundary between the major and minor tranquillizers, since chlorpromazine or fluphenazine may be used to counter anxiety in neurotic reactions, while a minor tranquillizer may be used as an adjunct to treatment of patients suffering from the major psychoses. There is quite a range of both types of tranquillizer, but most doctors restrict use to those with which they are familiar.

The major tranquillizers sometimes produce unpleasant side-effects, including muscle rigidity, tremors, salivation and a mask-like face and shuffling gait. When these side-effects arise the dose is usually reduced or the drug stopped, but sometimes another drug is given to counter them. Drugs in this category include benzhexol (Artane), orphenadrine hydrochloride (Disipal), or procyclidine (Kemadrin).

Sedatives and hypnotics   Of all the drugs presently in use, sedatives and hypnotics are perhaps the most over-prescribed and ill-advisedly used. In spite of warnings, exhortations and demonstrations of their potential dangers, too many people are still prescribed too many sedatives. Barbiturates are the most frequently abused and carry the greatest dangers. If a sedative is required it is safer to use preparations such as trichloral, dichloralphenazone (Welldorm), nitrazepam (Mogodon), or one of the antidepressants with sedative characteristics.

Antidepressants   There are now a large number of anti-depressants on the market, most of which fall into three main groups: the monoamine-oxidase inhibitors, the tricyclics and the quadracyclics. Examples of the first group are phenelzine (Nardil), isocarboxazid (Marplan) and tranylcypromine (Parnate). Examples of tricyclics are amitriptyline (Tryptizol,

Saroten and its long-acting form Lentizol), nortriptyline (Aventyl), protriptyline (Concordin), imipramine (Tofranil) and desipramine (Pertofran). The quadracyclics have only recently been introduced; one example is mianserin hydrochloride (Bolvidon, Norval).

Opinions differ about the use of monoamine-oxidase inhibitors but some psychiatrists consider that they are particularly effective in the treatment of neurotic depression, while the tricyclics are better suited to the treatment of endogenous or psychotic depression. The disadvantage of using monoamine-oxidase inhibitors is that they cannot be used at the same time as certain other drugs, including adrenalin, the amphetamines, ephedrine, tricyclic anti-depressants, narcotics, analgesics, anti-Parkinsonism drugs, sympathetic neurone blockers, ganglion blockers, and thiazides and similar oral diuretics. Certain foods which contain amines or amine precursors such as cheese, Bovril, Marmite and young broad beans with pods cannot be eaten by patients who are taking a monoamine-oxidase inhibitor. Because of these restrictions many patients cannot be given monoamine-oxidase inhibitors; they may need the incompatible drugs in a future emergency or fail to observe the dietary restrictions. Obviously, this does not mean that monoamine-oxidase inhibitors can never be used, rather that the number of patients who can be treated with them is limited. One important factor is the patient's ability and motivation carefully to observe the prohibitions or to allow someone else to do so on his or her behalf.

The most commonly used antidepressant is amitriptyline or its sustained release variant, Lentizol. Many people suffering from depression are also agitated, and it used to be common practice to prescribe both an antidepressant and a tranquillizer. This is rarely necessary with amitriptyline since it has tranquillizing properties. If the patient is particularly withdrawn and apathetic, protriptyline (Concordin) may be the antidepressant chosen, while for the patient who experiences an element of agitation, but in whom amitriptyline produces too much sedation, nortriptyline (Aventyl) can be most useful. The normal dose range of amitriptyline and nortriptyline is 25–50 mg twice daily; of proptriptyline,

10–20 mg twice daily; of Lentizol, 50–100 mg at night. If one preparation, in a reasonable dose, fails to work, it is better to change to another preparation than to increase the amount to possibly toxic levels. The dose range for mianserin hydrochloride (Bolvidon, Norval) is 10–20 mg taken twice to three times a day.

Some years ago lithium carbonate (Camcolit) was introduced as a treatment for mania. There is good evidence that this preparation can be effective in the treatment of depression and that it can be an effective prophylactic agent to prevent recurring attacks. Lithium carbonate is effective within a narrow range of concentration in the blood, below which it is ineffective and above which it may produce serious toxic effects, so if it is used it is essential that blood levels are monitored regularly and the dose suitably altered in response.

The first rule in the treatment of mental illness is that what is done should never make the patient's condition worse, nor in any way further erode his or her feelings of dignity, individuality and humanity. Most effective help depends upon the degree of understanding, sympathy and respect shown towards the patient by the therapist. Clearly there are no magic solutions to mental illness, and in the present state of knowledge, any treatment that is not harmful is worthy of consideration.

5 The Mental Health Act of 1959

The best-known legislation relating to mental illness is the Mental Health Act of 1959. This Act repealed the Lunacy and Mental Treatment Acts and Mental Deficiency Acts and replaced them with legislation that attempted to make the treatment, care and support of the mentally ill less a legal and more a medical and social responsibility. Obviously legal involvement remained, but this was intended to be far less prominent than previously.

The Act is made up of nine parts and eight schedules; this chapter will be concerned chiefly with section 5 of part 1 and part 4, since these deal with informal and compulsory admission to hospital and guardianship and thus have the greatest bearing upon mentally ill people unless they have been involved in some kind of criminal activity. Where appropriate I will mention the suggested reforms presented in the 1981 Mental Health (Amendment) Act.

The informal patient

Section 5 subsection 1 of the Mental Health Act 1959 states:

> Nothing in this Act shall be construed as preventing a patient who requires treatment for mental disorder from being admitted to any hospital or mental nursing home in pursuance of arrangements made in that behalf and without any application, order or direction rendering him liable to be detained under this Act, or from remaining in any hospital or mental nursing home in pursuance of such arrangements after he has ceased to be so liable to be detained.

Subsection 2 of this section states:

> In the case of an infant who has attained the age of sixteen years and is capable of expressing his own wishes, any such arrangements as are mentioned in the foregoing subsection may be made, carried out and determined notwithstanding any right of custody or control vested by law in his parent or guardian.

Section 5 contains the only specific references within the

Mental Health Act to informal status. The intention of the Act was that the majority of patients would be admitted informally, a substantial change in the law. Prior to the 1959 Act, patients admitted to mental institutions were admitted either compulsorily or as so-called 'voluntary patients'. Even now there is confusion between the concepts of voluntary patient and informal patient. Voluntary patients under the old legislation had to state specifically that they wished to enter a mental hospital and sign documents to testify to this. These documents stated clearly that while voluntary patients were able to leave hospital if they wished, they would have to give three days' notice. Thus, voluntary patients had to express a positive wish to enter the hospital and they were also made aware that they could not leave on the instant, but had to give notice. It was also indicated that other action might be taken during this period of notice if the authorities considered that patients should not leave. In fact, a voluntary patient could be certified during this period, if that was the decision of the medical and legal authorities.

Informal patients under the present legislation do not have to express a positive wish to enter a hospital or sign any forms. Neither do they have to give notice of wanting to leave. In theory they can declare their intention to do so at any time and cannot be prevented. However, section 30 of the Act still makes it possible for an informal patient to be detained compulsorily, if he says he is leaving and the responsible doctor judges this inadvisable.

It has been said that a patient who enters a mental hospital, psychiatric unit in a general hospital or mental nursing home informally does this in the same way that any other patient enters a hospital. The informal patient may ask to come into hospital or, on the other hand, may be sent there and can still be admitted informally if she does not specifically refuse. For example, a depressed patient may be seen in her home – either by her family doctor or by a psychiatrist invited by the family doctor – and advised to enter hospital. She may not respond to this suggestion, but if she has not refused to go she may then be admitted, provided of course that she passively submits to the arrangements. The situation is similar to that of a physically ill person who does not respond to the suggestion that he should be in hospital and whose lack of reaction is taken as consent. Provided that he yields to the process of admission, he is assumed to be in hospital of his own free will. Whether or not this is a satisfactory arrangement is a matter for debate, but this is how informal admissions occur, be they to psychiatric establishments and general hospitals because of mental ill health, or to general hospitals because of physical disorders.

From this example we can see that the Act attempted to make the treatment of mental illness similar, as far as legal status is concerned, to the treatment of physical disorders. Prior to the Act it had been possible to obtain treatment for mental disorders on the same footing as for physical disorders, but the facilities were limited to a few beds in teaching hospitals and one small voluntary hospital on the south coast.

The informal patient in hospital

So far we have seen that a patient may enter a mental hospital or other type of psychiatric establishment in the same way as a patient enters a general hospital. However, after admission to hospital this similarity between the two begins to break down. Patients in non-psychiatric hospitals can discharge themselves at any time and cannot be prevented legally from so doing. The psychiatric patient can be prevented by the powers contained in section 30 of the Act, which states:

(1) An application for the admission of a patient to a hospital may be made under this Part of the Act —
   (a) in any case, notwithstanding that the patient is already an inpatient in that hospital, not being liable to be detained in pursuance of an application under this Part of the Act.

Subsection 2 further states:

If, in the case of a patient who is an inpatient in a hospital, not being liable to be detained therein under this Part of this Act, it appears to the medical practitioner in charge of the treatment of the patient that an application ought to be made under this Part of this Act for the admission of the patient to hospital, he may furnish to the managers a report in writing to that effect; and in any such case the patient may be detained in the hospital for a period of three days beginning with the day on which the report is so furnished.

The Mental Health (Amendment) Bill recommends some significant changes to the current Act. They include giving the right to use section 30 to doctors other than the medical practitioner in charge of the patient's treatment, and suggesting that certain nurses should be empowered to detain a patient for a period of up to six hours.

An example of the use of section 30 is given below.

Miss Jean Martin became depressed and consulted her family doctor. He tried a combination of counselling and antidepressant drugs, with some effect, but she still remained depressed and he referred her to a psychiatric outpatient department. The psychiatrist who saw her thought she would benefit from a period in hospital, and she agreed to this. She was admitted to a psychiatric unit in a general hospital. Following admission she became more depressed and talked of killing herself. One Sunday afternoon she suddenly announced that she wished to leave the hospital. Her psychiatrist was informed and came to see her. He tried to persuade her to stay, but she demanded to leave. The psychiatrist considered that she was very depressed and ran the risk of attempting to kill herself. He decided to keep her in hospital using the powers provided under section 30 of the Mental Health Act. He completed the appropriate form and told the patient and the staff on the ward that she was detained compulsorily.

The next day, Monday, he again asked her if she would remain in hospital and she again said that she wanted to leave. It was decided that she needed to be detained for a period, and her family doctor came to see her. An application was made by a local authority social worker for detention under section 25 of the Mental Health Act, and the family doctor and the psychiatrist completed the two medical recommendations. Following further treatment she recovered and finally left hospital, though returning as an outpatient.

In the same way as a patient may be admitted informally if he does not expressly voice an objection, he can be detained indefinitely in hospital unless he states specifically that he wishes to leave. This is again similar to the situation of patients in general hospitals, except that the mentally ill or mentally handicapped patient may have particular problems in making his wishes known, and so may have a strong desire to leave even though he has never asked to do so. This problem also causes dispute; I shall mention it again in chapter 13.

The 1959 Act makes little distinction, once patients are in hospital, between the rights of those admitted as informal patients and those admitted compulsorily. Informal patients are therefore under the same legal restrictions as formal patients – that is, people admitted compulsorily – as regards court access, voting, obtaining a driving licence, sending and receiving mail, and receiving pocket money. These matters will be considered in detail in chapter 8. The 1959 Act intended that all patients, regardless of their legal status, should be treated purely on the basis of their medical condition. This is clearly an important legal point.

The concept of informal status was and is an important one, having played a significant part in the normalization and liberalization of psychiatric care. However, it does have drawbacks which require remedies, though these must be approached with care so as not to destroy the original concept. While it was the hope and intention of the Act that the great majority of mentally ill people would be treated informally, it was understood that this would not be possible for some of them. Five sections of the Act are concerned with compulsory admission or retention in hospital. These sections are found in part 4 of the Act.

Admission for observation

Section 25 of the Act makes it possible for a patient to be admitted to hospital and detained there for a period not exceeding twenty-eight days from the day of admittance.

An application for a patient's admission under this section of the Act may be made on the grounds:

(a) that he is suffering from mental disorder of a nature or degree which warrants the detention of the patient in a hospital under observation (with or without other medical treatment) for at least a limited period; and

(b) that he ought to be so detained in the interests of his own health or safety or with a view to the protection of other persons.

An application for the admission of the patient must be made by either the nearest relative of the patient or a social worker specifically invested with the powers previously held by a local authority mental welfare officer. It is always preferable that a social worker makes the application; firstly this prevents the nearest relative's involvement in an action that may damage his or her relationship with the patient, and secondly the social worker will be more experienced and better able to protect the patient against inappropriate use of the powers contained under this section and invested in the two doctors. The definition of nearest relative will be considered later in this chapter.

The application for admission for observation must be made on an official form (see Appendix, form 1). The application needs to be founded on the recommendation, again written on prescribed forms, of two medical practitioners. The forms used here may be either a joint medical recommendation, in which both doctors use the same form, or two separate forms (see Appendix, forms 2 and 3). Each must state that the patient is suffering from a mental disorder that warrants his or her detention, and that he or she ought to be detained in the interests of his or her own health and safety, or with a view to the protection of others. Each also needs to state that informal admission is not appropriate in the present case.

One of the doctors concerned must have a special knowledge of psychiatry and be recognized as such by being approved under section 28 of the Act by the Secretary of State for Health and Social Security. In the past this approval was given by local authorities, but since the reorganization of the Health Service the duty has passed to the Secretary of State. The other doctor should preferably be the patient's family doctor, but can be any medical practitioner. Usually the doctor with a special knowledge of psychiatry would be the consultant psychiatrist under whose care the patient would be placed when admitted to hospital. However, nothing in the Act states that this should be so, and in fact the specialist doctor can be a family practitioner (though not the patient's own doctor, and preferably not a member of the same practice) or any psychiatrist who has been appropriately recognized.

The two doctors recommending admission must both see the patient, though not necessarily at the same time; the interval between their examinations must not, however, exceed seven days. The recommendation must be signed on or before the date of application, which in turn must fall within seven days of the patient's examination. If he or she is to be admitted to a National Health Service hospital, one but not both of the doctors may be drawn from its staff. If the patient is to be admitted to a private mental nursing home neither medical recommendation can be made by doctors who work there. This also applies when patients are admitted to private wards in National Health Service hospitals.

A medical recommendation cannot be made by any of the following: the applicant, i.e. the person making the application for compulsory admission; a partner of the applicant, or of a practitioner who is providing another medical recommendation for the purposes of the same application; a person employed as an assistant by the applicant; a person who receives or has an interest in the receipt of any payment made on account of the maintenance of the patient; or any relative of the patient.

Patients admitted to hospital under this section can be allowed to leave at any time if this is the decision of the psychiatrist responsible for their care in hospital. They can also leave at the end of twenty-eight days, unless they have been dealt with before then under section 26 of the Act. At the end of twenty-eight days they can remain as informal patients if that is their wish.

There is some dispute as to whether a patient admitted for observation can be given medical treatment against his or her wishes. Section 25, paragraph 2a does allow for 'the detention of the patient in a hospital under observation (with or without medical treatment) for at least a limited period'. This may or may not permit the use of compulsory treatment, but in practice patients admitted to hospital under this section are frequently given treatment against their wishes, and it would be extremely difficult to deal with such patients in hospital if compulsory treatment was not allowed under any circumstances.

The Mental Health (Amendment) Bill contains an important reform of this section, and also changes the term 'admission for observation' to 'admission for assessment'. Section 3(4b) of the Bill states:

A patient who is admitted to a hospital in pursuance of an application for admission for assessment may apply to a Mental Health Review Tribunal within the period of 14 days, beginning with the day on which he is so admitted.

Section 3(2) states that

Before or within a reasonable time after an application for the admission of a patient for assessment is made by a Mental Welfare Officer that officer shall take such steps as are practicable to inform the person (if any) appearing to be the nearest relative of the patient, that the application is to be made, or has been made, and of the power of the nearest relative under Section 47 of this Act, to discharge the patient.

Admission for treatment

Section 26 of the Act enables a patient to be admitted to hospital and detained there for a period of up to one year, provided there is an appropriate application supported by two medical recommendations.

The grounds for admission under this section are that the patient is suffering from a mental disorder: for patients of any age this comprises mental illness or severe subnormality, and additionally, for patients younger than twenty-one, psychopathic disorder or subnormality. The disorder must be of a nature or degree that warrants the patient's detention in a hospital for medical treatment, either in the interests of his or her own health or safety, or for the protection of others. It follows that a patient over twenty-one diagnosed as having some psychopathic disorder or subnormality cannot be compulsorily detained in hospital simply because of these conditions, but must be found to be suffering from another mental illness before he can be detained. This absurd state of affairs means that diagnoses sometimes have to be modified to conform to the Act's requirements. For instance, a patient previously diagnosed as suffering from a psychopathic disorder might be reclassified as a victim of simple schizophrenia.

The conditions governing the medical applications are similar to those under section 25, except that the doctors must give reasons for their diagnosis on the appropriate form (see Appendix, form 4). There is a further significant difference: as in section 25 the application can be made either by the nearest relative or by a social worker recognized as having the powers of a mental welfare officer, but in section 26 the social worker cannot make an application if the nearest relative objects. Generally speaking the patient cannot be admitted to hospital if the nearest relative does object, but it is possible to overcome the objection under certain circumstances by applying to the County Court to have another person appointed as the nearest relative (section 52). This may be any relative with whom the patient is residing, or a social worker with the powers of a mental welfare officer. There are special forms for application by the nearest relative and by the mental welfare officer (see Appendix, forms 5 and 6).

A patient detained under this section of the Act can be released from hospital at any time by the consultant psychiatrist responsible for his care or by the managers of the hospital. He can also be released on the demand of the nearest relative so long as this status has not been lost within the meaning of the Act. However, the consultant psychiatrist responsible for the patient's care can bar this form of discharge. If the nearest relative asks for the patient's release he has to give not less than seventy-two hours' notice in writing to the managers of the hospital, during which interval the responsible doctor can submit a report barring discharge. This is stated under section 48 of the Act:

(2) An order for the discharge of a patient who is liable to be detained in a hospital shall not be made by his nearest relative except after giving not less than seventy-two hours' notice in writing to the managers of the hospital; and if, within seventy-two hours after such notice has been given, the responsible medical officer furnishes to the managers a report certifying that in the opinion of that officer the patient, if discharged, would be likely to act in a manner dangerous to other persons or to himself, —

    (a) any order for the discharge of the patient made by that relative in pursuance of the notice shall be of no effect; and

    (b) no further order for the discharge of the patient shall be made by that relative during the period of six months beginning with the date of the report.

(3) In any case where a report under subsection (2) of this section is furnished in respect of a patient, the managers shall cause the nearest relative of the patient to be informed, and that relative may, within the period of twenty-eight days beginning with the day on which he is so informed, apply to a Mental Health Review Tribunal in respect of the patient.

A special document is used by the doctor wishing to bar discharge by the nearest relative (see Appendix, form 7). The patient can be released at the direction of a Mental Health Review Tribunal. At the end of a year, either the patient must be released, or he or she must agree to become an informal patient, or the order must be extended by the responsible medical officer — the consultant psychiatrist responsible for the patient's care — who must provide the managers of the hospital with an application for the extension of the order by a further year. The order may be extended on a yearly basis without limit.

The following case illustrates some of the points I have been discussing.

At the age of twenty Mr Tom Osborne became mentally ill. His family doctor referred him to a psychiatric outpatient department, where he was seen by a psychiatrist who diagnosed schizophrenia. Medication was prescribed but Mr Osborne's condition did not improve. He became more withdrawn and solitary and people often heard him talking strangely. His conversation was disjointed and unintelligible and he occasionally heard voices. He was advised to enter hospital and agreed to do so, but after being there for two weeks he left without telling anyone. He returned to his parents and refused to go back to the hospital. He now spent most of his time in his bedroom. Sometimes he would become angry for no apparent reason, and during one of these fits of temper he broke the bedroom window, cutting his arm. His doctor was called and said that he should be in hospital. He refused to go informally and was admitted under section 25 of the Mental Health Act. When the compulsory powers under this section expired he stayed on as an informal patient, but within three weeks left the hospital again without telling anyone. Not returning to his parents' home this time, he started instead to sleep rough. Three months later he did go back to his parents, dirty and emaciated. Again he was seen by his family doctor, who considered that he should return to the mental hospital, but again he refused firmly. A consultant psychiatrist visited him and decided that he needed prolonged treatment in hospital. It was thought that if he did not go to hospital there was a danger he might die from self-neglect. An application was made by a local authority social worker, with his parents' approval, for his admission to hospital for treatment under section 26 of the Act. His family doctor completed one medical recommendation and the consultant psychiatrist the other. Following this Mr Osborne was admitted to hospital. After prolonged treatment he was discharged to a hostel where he was able to find employment and settle down to work and hostel life.

In the case of section 26, the Mental Health (Amendment) Bill does away with the question of psychopathic disorder or subnormality in patients over 21, and substitutes for the present grounds for application the following:

4 (2) (a) That [the patient] is suffering from mental illness, severe mental handicap, psychopathic disorder, or mental handicap, being a mental disorder of a nature or degree which makes it appropriate for him to receive medical treatment in hospital and

   (b) In the case of psychopathic disorder, or mental handicap, that such treatment is likely to alleviate, or prevent a deterioration of his condition and

   (c) That it is necessary for the health or safety of the patient, or for the protection of other persons that he should receive such treatment and that it cannot be provided unless he is detained under this Section.

There are also minor changes in the conditions of medical recommendations, including a reduction in the period between the two doctors' examinations (if these do not occur together) from seven to five days, and allowance for the two doctors to be both employed by the same hospital, provided that one of them works there for less than half of the time which he is bound by contract to devote to work in the Health Service, and that where one of them is a consultant the other does not work in a grade under that consultant's direction.

Admission for observation in case of emergency
Section 29 of the Act deals with compulsory admission in an emergency. An application under this section may be made either by a social worker with the powers of a mental welfare officer or by any relative of the patient, and the application need only be supported by one medical recommendation, which can be given by any medical practitioner, but preferably

by the patient's family doctor. There is an appropriate form for applications under this section (see Appendix, form 8). The medical recommendation for an admission under section 29 is made on the same form as the first part of an admission under section 25 (see Appendix, form 3).

This section of the Act is for use only when urgent admission to hospital is necessary and it is not possible to obtain a second medical recommendation, as laid down under sections 25 and 26 of the Act. A patient can be detained in hospital for three days only under this section. While the patient is in hospital, however, and before this period has elapsed, a second medical recommendation may be made by a doctor recognized as having a special knowledge of psychiatry, and if the appropriate conditions are observed the patient may then be detained under the powers contained in section 25 or section 26 of the Act. Section 29 should in fact be used only rarely, since there are few emergencies so urgent that it is impossible to obtain the opinion of a doctor with a special knowledge of psychiatry.

In sections 25 and 26, a patient can be removed to hospital within fourteen days, beginning on the date when he or she was last examined by the appropriate medical practitioners. In an emergency application (section 29), admission to hospital must occur within a period of three days from the day when the patient was examined by the practitioner who is making the medical recommendation.

Evidence suggests that section 29 is often misused; there are patients who would be willing to enter hospital informally but who are admitted compulsorily, either because of the doctor's misunderstanding of the Act or because of the belief that using this section will force a hospital to accept a patient where there might have been resistance to an informal admission. This subject will be discussed further in chapter 13. Here is a case which demonstrates the appropriate use of this type of compulsion.

Mrs Ann Curtiss had been feeling depressed for some time, but had not consulted her doctor. Her feelings of misery increased, she found it difficult to concentrate or do her housework, and she had no interest in food. Her sleep was disturbed: she found that she could go to sleep fairly easily, but tended to wake up in the early hours, when she felt worse than ever and could not get back to sleep. Early one morning she awoke feeling utterly miserable. She went to the bathroom and began to swallow aspirins. Fortunately her husband, woken by her movements, and worried, followed her to the bathroom and managed to prevent her taking more than a few aspirins. He had to struggle but did not hurt her. He telephoned his doctor who came out and saw her. He considered that she was suffering from a severe depression and would be in danger of attempting to take her life again unless she was admitted to hospital. He suggested to her that it would be best if she entered hospital, but she refused adamantly, saying that she would be all right at home. The doctor decided that she needed to be admitted to hospital compulsorily and that this was urgent. He telephoned the duty social worker, who saw the patient and agreed with him. By now the doctor had contacted the local psychiatric hospital, whose duty doctor had agreed to accept the patient. The social worker made an application for admission under section 29 of the Mental Health Act, and the doctor completed the medical recommendation.

Mrs Curtiss was admitted to hospital, and after two days agreed to remain as an informal patient. She stayed in hospital for six weeks, during which she was treated for depression and made an excellent recovery.

The Mental Health (Amendment) Bill contains significant reforms bearing on this section. In the principal Act any relative of the patient can make an application; the Bill proposes this be changed to the nearest relative. It also states that the person making the application must have seen the patient personally in the previous twenty-four hours, as distinct from fourteen days in the principal Act. The patient should also be admitted within the twenty-four hours following the application, as compared with fourteen days in the current legislation. These changes are sensible corrections to the principal Act, which allows emergency admissions to take place in anything but emergency time. Under the principal Act up to a month can elapse between the applicant seeing the patient and the patient being admitted to hospital.

Mentally disordered persons found in public places
Section 136 of the Act empowers police constables to remove to a place of safety any person who is found in a place to which the public has access and who appears to be suffering from a mental disorder and to be in need of control. This

removal must be justified in the interest of that person or for the protection of others. He or she can be detained for not longer than seventy-two hours for examination by a medical practitioner and for an interview with a social worker with the powers of a mental welfare officer. Precisely what constitutes a place of safety is not clearly stated; in practice it is usually assumed to be a psychiatric hospital or psychiatric unit. However, detention can take place in a police station, hostel or any other accommodation that provides the necessary degree of safety and is willing to accept the detainee. An example of the working of section 136 follows.

A police officer came upon an elderly man who, clad only in underpants, was dancing about on the grassed centre of a busy roundabout. He was singing lustily, and when approached by the police officer said that he had discovered the secret of living for ever. He offered to demonstrate his immortality by rushing into the traffic without getting killed. The policeman decided he was either drunk or mentally ill, and inclined toward the latter. Using the provisions of section 136 of the Mental Health Act, he took the man to the local police station, where he was seen by the police surgeon, who decided that he was mentally ill. A psychiatrist was called and diagnosed hypomania. The man was admitted to the local mental hospital under section 25 of the Mental Health Act.

The nearest relative
The nearest relative is an important person, particularly in relation to section 26 of the Act. The term is defined in section 49, which states that a relative means any of the following: husband or wife, son or daughter, father, mother, brother or sister, grandparent, grandchild, uncle or aunt, nephew or niece. The nearest relative will be the first one mentioned in the list. An adopted person is treated as the child of his or her adopted parents, and an illegitimate person is treated as the legitimate child of his or her mother. In defining nearest relative, relatives of whole blood are preferred to their half-blood equivalents and the elder is preferred over the younger relative, regardless of sex.

The Amendment Bill makes the father and mother equal in the above hierarchy and gives preference to the relative or relatives with whom patients are living, or were living prior to their admission to hospital.

In the principal Act, the nearest relative had to be resident within the United Kingdom. The Bill amends this to the United Kingdom, the Channel Islands, or the Isle of Man.

When a patient is admitted to hospital compulsorily he or she loses certain rights, but retains others. The rights of patients in hospital, whether admitted informally or under compulsion, will be considered in chapter 8, along with the function and powers of Mental Health Review Tribunals, who are concerned with applications for release from compulsorily detained patients.

Guardianship
Sections 33 and 34 of the Act make it possible to place someone under the guardianship of the local authority or of any named adult. The guardian is endowed with the same powers and responsibilities as a father has in respect of a child under the age of fourteen. A guardianship order resembles the provision for compulsory admission for treatment under section 26 of the Act, except that hospital admission is not involved; the patient simply remains under the control of the appointed guardian. The order is effective for one year, but like section 26 can be extended indefinitely. Applications and recommendations are made on the appropriate forms (see Appendix, forms 9 and 10). Like those detained under section 26, people placed under guardianship orders are allowed to make applications to the Mental Health Review Tribunal.

Guardianship orders are not extensively used except for dealing with mentally handicapped people. Some people advocate that this provision should be more frequently used, to give patients the chance to receive treatment under controlled conditions while still remaining in the community. One major drawback is that both local authorities and individuals are reluctant to take on the responsibility involved, and as a result there is a tendency to choose other compulsory powers to obtain hospital admission instead.

The Amendment Bill limits a guardianship order to those over the age of sixteen and abolishes the age limit of twenty-one in relation to psychopathic disorder or subnormality, so that an application may be made in respect of 'mental illness, severe mental handicap, psychopathic disorder, or mental handicap'. Where the principal Act refers to 'the interests of the patient', the Amendment Bill substitutes 'the interests of the welfare of the patient'.

Powers to enter a patient's house

Section 22 of the Act states that a social worker with the powers previously held by the mental welfare officer may at any reasonable time enter and inspect any premises where a mentally disordered person is living (except hospitals) within the relevant local authority area, if he or she has reasonable cause to believe that that person is not under proper care. If the social worker is denied access to the home of a mentally ill person who lives alone or who is believed to be subjected to ill treatment or neglect, the provisions in section 135 make it possible to obtain a warrant to search the house and, if necessary, to remove the patient to a place of safety. Evidence must be submitted to a Justice of the Peace, who will issue a warrant if satisfied that there is a mentally disordered person in the house and that admission has been refused. The warrant authorizes any constable named in it to enter the premises, by force if need be, and remove the patient. The constable must be accompanied by a medical practitioner and any person authorized for the purpose under the Mental Health Act.

After the patient has been removed from the house he or she must be taken to a place of safety, where he or she can be detained for up to three days. During this time the patient can be dealt with if necessary under the sections of the Act that provide for compulsory admission and detention in hospital. Section 135 defines a place of safety as:

> residential accommodation provided by a local authority under Part 3 of the National Health Service Act 1946, or under Part 3 of the National Assistance Act 1948, a hospital as defined by this Act, a police station, a mental nursing home or residential home for mentally disordered persons, or any other suitable place, the occupier of which is willing, temporarily, to receive the patient.

The powers provided by section 135 are rarely used but necessary at times. Carrying them out sometimes presents practical problems: it is hard to prove that the occupant of a house is mentally disordered without seeing him or her, for instance. Nevertheless, such difficulties should be sustained; to ease them would be to set the liberty of the individual at risk.

6 The Mental Health Act and Mentally Ill Offenders

When someone suspected of a crime is found to be unfit to stand trial or to plead, he or she cannot be convicted but instead must be compulsorily committed to a mental hospital or special hospital, as we shall see in chapter 7. Many people charged with criminal offences, however, are fit to stand trial and to plead even though they are suffering from mental illness. Part 5 of the Mental Health Act 1959 empowers the courts to deal with such cases, and also makes provision for convicts to be transferred from prisons to mental hospitals or units if they are suffering from certain mental disorders.

Powers of magistrates
If someone is convicted in a Magistrates' Court of an offence that is punishable with imprisonment on summary conviction, but is found to be mentally ill, the magistrates are empowered under section 60 of the Mental Health Act to order admission to and detention in hospital, or to place him or her under the guardianship of the local authority or of a person approved by it. Section 60 paragraph 2 allows a Magistrates' Court to make an order without convicting the defendant, provided that the court is satisfied that he or she committed the offence and that the case meets the requirements set down in this section for making an order.

The conditions for making an order under section 60 are similar to those that empower doctors to admit a patient to hospital compulsorily under section 26 of the Act, which, of course, concerns non-offenders. Written or oral evidence from two medical practitioners must be provided, at least one of whom must be approved by the Secretary of State for the purposes of section 28 of the Act as having special experience in the diagnosis and treatment of mental disorders. In practice, written evidence is always required, though it need not be supported by proof of the signature or qualifications of the practitioner signing the report. However the court may ask the practitioner to give oral evidence. Since an order under section 60 is made by a court it is not appropriate to present an application for admission as it is under sections 29, 25 and 26. The medical evidence must be given on special forms that include a statement establishing mental illness and describing the symptoms and form of illness, together with the reasons why it is thought that the mental illness is of a nature or degree which warrants the detention of the patient in hospital for medical treatment. There are separate forms for mental illness, subnormality, severe subnormality and psychopathy, but apart from the specific mention of these categories they are substantially the same (see Appendix, forms 11 and 12).

If the accused is represented by counsel or by a solicitor, they must receive a copy of the report. If the accused is not represented, the substance of the report must be disclosed to him, or, if he is a child or young person, to his parent or guardian. He is allowed to have the practitioner called upon for oral evidence and he can then call his own evidence to refute it.

The court needs to be satisfied that the medical evidence proves that the offender is suffering from mental illness, psychopathic disorder, subnormality, or severe subnormality, and that the mental disorder is of a nature or degree which warrants his detention in a hospital for medical treatment, or his reception into guardianship as provided in the Act. The court must also have decided, taking into account all the circumstances including the nature of the offence, the character and past history of the offender, and the other available methods of dealing with him, that the most suitable way of settling the case is to make an order under this section. Such an order cannot be made unless the court is satisfied that arrangements have been made to admit the offender to hospital in the event of such an order being made by the court, and that this admission can occur within twenty-eight days from the date of the order. In the case of guardianship, the court must be sure that the local authority will accept the guardianship. If this order is used, the court is not allowed to pass sentence of imprisonment, impose a fine, or make a probation order in respect of the offence or offences concerned.

Once someone has been dealt with under section 60 of the Act and either admitted to hospital or taken into guardianship, the conditions of his detention are identical with those that apply under section 26 of part 4 of the Act and section 33 of the Act respectively. This means that the individual is initially detained in hospital for a year (renewable annually if appropriate medical evidence is given), or kept under guardianship. However, the psychiatrist responsible for his care in hospital can discharge the patient at any time, on his own responsibility, without reference to anyone else. But there are two significant differences between an order under section 26 and an order under section 60. Section 60 does not empower the nearest relative to discharge the patient, and the special provisions on the expiration and renewal of authority for detention (and for guardianship, in the case of psychopathic and subnormal patients) do not apply. The patient does, however, have the same rights to apply to a Mental Health Review Tribunal, which may decide to discharge the patient without reference to anyone else.

Thus someone dealt with under section 60 cannot have his discharge restricted by the court; to balance this, section 65 of the Act does give the courts powers to restrict the release of certain people. However, a Magistrates' Court is not permitted to use it, and if it decides that this legislation should be employed, it has to commit the defendant in custody to the Crown Court, which does have the power to place restrictions on his release. Section 68 of the Act empowers the Magistrates' Court to commit people to a hospital for detention awaiting the decision of the Crown Court.

Here is an example of the use of section 60 of the Mental Health Act.

Mr Augustus Tompkins went into a stationer's and asked to see the manager, who came over to speak to him by a counter that had cardboard box files on display. Mr Tompkins told the manager the shop in fact belonged to him, and had been given him by Churchill as a reward for his unique contribution to the Second World War. The manager, astonished, said 'You're talking rubbish, don't waste my time.' Mr Tompkins became annoyed and shouted abuse at the manager and knocked the stack of files onto the floor. He proceeded to jump up and down on them, all the while maintaining the flow of abuse.

The police were called and Mr Tompkins was arrested. The local magistrates before whom he appeared thought he was possibly mentally ill, and remanded him in custody for psychiatric reports. The prison medical officer saw him and then sought the opinion of a consultant psychiatrist. Mr Tompkins was found to be overactive and over-talkative; his conversation was disjointed and flitted from one topic to the next, a condition known as 'flight of ideas'. Mr Tompkins also had a number of grandiose delusions: he said he had been an important member of the underground movement in France whose exploits had secured the victory of the Allies, and as a reward Churchill had given him a chain of well-known stationery shops. He also claimed that he was superbly fit and could easily win the world heavyweight boxing championship. (In fact he was a rather thin, small man in his sixties.)

Hypomania was diagnosed, and it was recommended that Mr Tompkins should be dealt with under section 60 of the Mental Health Act so that he could be compulsorily admitted to a psychiatric hospital for treatment. The possibility of dealing with him under section 3 of the Criminal Justice Act 1948 was also considered. Mr Tompkins, however, insisted that he was well and did not need any treatment. He declared that there was no reason why he should be in prison, and as soon as he explained the facts of the matter to the magistrates they would release him and award him compensation. He appeared before the magistrates, who agreed to a section 60 order, and he was admitted to the local psychiatric hospital. Following treatment there he slowly recovered and was finally discharged six months later, to have his treatment followed up as an outpatient.

Powers of the Crown Court

The Crown Court may deal in the same way as a Magistrates' Court with an offender under section 60 of the Act, when the conditions I have previously described will apply. However, the Crown Court also has extra powers under section 65 of the Act. It may, on deciding that there is a risk that the accused will commit further offences if freed, and that his early release should be prevented for the protection of the public, order that he should be placed under the special restrictions set out in this section, either for a specified period or without limit of time. Before the powers of section 65 can be used, the offender must first be dealt with under section 60 of the Act, whose conditions must be applicable to his own case.

If a restriction order is to be made under section 65, at

least one of the medical practitioners who gave a recommendation under section 60 must now give oral evidence in court. If these powers are used, certain special restrictions then apply: none of the provisions of part 4 of the Act, concerned with the duration, renewal and expiration of authority for the detention of patients, are applicable, and the patient cannot apply for release to a Mental Health Review Tribunal, as is the case under part 4 of the Act, though the Home Secretary may seek the advice of the Mental Health Review Tribunal. In fact, people detained under this section can apply for their cases to be reviewed, but the Mental Health Review Tribunal can only make recommendations to the Home Secretary, and cannot order the patient's release. Only the Secretary of State can: grant leave of absence to the patient under section 39 of the Act; allow the transfer of the patient to another hospital or to guardianship, or permit the transfer of guardianship from one authority to another; or order the discharge of the patient. The Secretary of State has the power to recall the patient or take him into custody and return him to hospital at any time.

As we have seen, a restriction order can be made for a limited period or without limit of time. If the order is for a limited period, for example two years, the restriction is lifted once the time has elapsed and the patient can then be dealt with as if he were detained under section 26 of part 4 of the Act. In a restriction order without limit of time, the restriction applies until the patient's death unless the Secretary of State uses the powers conferred upon him to discharge the patient. The Secretary of State may do this at any time, and the discharge may be absolute and without restriction, or subject to certain conditions. Conditional discharge may involve the patient living at a specific address, regularly attending an outpatient clinic and submitting to other forms of supervision. It also means that the Secretary of State may order the patient to return to hospital at any time. If he has been discharged conditionally and is re-admitted to a mental hospital, he cannot later be discharged without the Secretary of State's permission even if the re-admission was at his own request.

It can be seen that a restriction order under section 65 restricts not only the patient, but also the responsible psychiatrist. Under section 60 of the Act, the court hands over the future care, treatment and detention of the patient to the responsible psychiatrist, or perhaps more correctly, to the managers of the hospital where he or she works. Under section 65, the responsible psychiatrist and the managers of the hospital are restricted in their handling of the patient; the aim of this section of the Act was to protect the public in general against the inappropriate release of patients from hospital. It is becoming increasingly common for courts to place restrictions on the patient without limit of time when they use section 65, but this does not mean that shorter periods of restriction are not possible or advisable.

The following case illustrates the kind of circumstances that can result in the use of section 65.

John Smith suffered from schizophrenia, and one of his main symptoms was a delusional belief that certain people, whom he described as the 'Scraggs', were trying to injure him in various ways, even kill him if they could. His illness had begun in his early twenties; he had been treated in hospital on several occasions and had made some improvement while there, but the symptoms soon recurred once he had left. When he was thirty-two he was once again discharged from hospital, and as well as being seen regularly as an outpatient, he was visited at home by a social worker. In the past he had occasionally attacked people, believing each time that they were members of the 'Scraggs'. One afternoon the social worker went to visit Mr Smith at home; when he opened the door for the visitor, he was holding a large carving knife in his hand. He yelled abuse at the social worker, accusing him of being a 'Scragg', and stabbed him in the chest. Fortunately, two men were passing and went to the social worker's assistance. The police and an ambulance were called. Mr Smith was arrested and the social worker taken to hospital where he had an emergency operation, later to recover slowly from a grave chest injury. Mr Smith was committed to the Crown Court after appearing at the Magistrates' Court, and a recommendation was made that he should be seen by a psychiatrist. The prison medical officer and a consultant psychiatrist saw Mr Smith while he was on remand in prison, and both concluded that he was suffering from paranoid schizophrenia and should be dealt with under a hospital order, with a restriction placed on his discharge. They also recommended that he be admitted to a special hospital for treatment. When Mr Smith appeared in the Crown Court, the judge agreed that he should be dealt with under section 60 of the Mental Health Act, and used section 65 to place a restriction on his discharge without limit of time. Following this court appearance he was admitted to a special hospital.

Transfer of prisoners to hospital or guardianship
A person serving a prison sentence may be transferred from prison to hospital under section 72 of the Act if the Secretary of State is satisfied by the evidence of two medical practitioners, one of whom must have a special knowledge of psychiatry, that he or she is suffering from a mental illness, psychopathic disorder, subnormality, or severe subnormality, and that the mental disorder is of a nature or degree that warrants the detention of the patient in a hospital for medical treatment. As with the medical reports given under section 60, there are separate forms for mental illness, subnormality, severe subnormality and psychopathy (see Appendix, forms 13 and 14).

A person transferred to hospital in this way can be kept there compulsorily until either he is thought fit enough to return to prison, or the sentence he was serving expires. If the patient is still in hospital when his prison sentence expires, he can be further detained in hospital under section 26 of the Mental Health Act, provided that the required conditions are fulfilled. While a prisoner is in hospital under section 72, he is not entitled to any remissions of sentence that would apply if he was in prison.

The following case provides an example of the use of this section.

Alexander McGuire was sentenced to five years' imprisonment for robbery. He had been involved with the law prior to this sentence and had also had treatment in a psychiatric hospital for severe depression. While serving the five-year sentence he again suffered severe depression. His actions and thoughts slowed down, he lost his appetite, found it difficult to sleep and proclaimed that he was a wicked, sinful man who ought to be killed. He said he could not eat because he did not deserve food, and should not be offered the comfort of a prison because he was unworthy even of that. Treatment was started in prison using anti-depressant drugs, but his condition did not improve. He was losing weight rapidly and it was judged that he needed hospital treatment. The psychiatrist who was called to visit him diagnosed severe depression and recommended that he be transferred to hospital for a course of electro-convulsive treatment. The prison medical officer and the psychiatrist submitted the appropriate medical recommendations under section 72 of the Mental Health Act, and he was admitted to the local psychiatric hospital. He received a course of electroconvulsive therapy and was encouraged to involve himself in the occupational and recreational activities of the hospital. He made a reasonably rapid recovery; after being in hospital for about five months he was considered well enough to return to prison, and he duly went back to complete his sentence.

Section 74 of the Act empowers the Secretary of State to place a restriction on the discharge of prisoners transferred under section 72, similar to that provided by section 65 of the Act. To quote this section 'a direction under this Section (in this Act referred to as a direction restricting discharge) shall have the like effect as an order restricting the discharge of the patient made under the said Section 65'.

The Mental Health (Amendment) Bill proposes a number of changes to part 5 of the principal Act. It sets out to implement proposals made by the Butler Committee for remands to hospital for medical reports and for treatment and assessment in order to determine whether a hospital order would be a suitable way of disposing of a case. It suggests that remands to hospital for medical reports and for treatment should last for up to twenty-eight days and be renewable for up to twelve weeks. If there is reason to suspect that an accused is suffering from any of the four categories of mental disorder, a remand could be made on medical evidence for a medical report; remands for treatment, on the other hand, would only be made in cases of mental illness or severe mental handicap. In both cases, remand to hospital would only be considered when bail was not possible.

An interim hospital order, to allow assessment of whether a hospital order would be appropriate, could be made for twelve weeks, renewable for up to six months if the court was satisfied by evidence from two doctors that the convicted person was suffering from mental illness, psychopathic disorder, mental handicap or severe mental handicap, and that a hospital order might be appropriate.

An order could only be made under section 60 if the person in question is convicted before the Crown Court of an offence punishable with imprisonment. Remands for treatment would carry the further condition that they could only be made if 'treatment is likely to alleviate, or prevent a deterioration of, his condition'. This condition would also apply to the transfer of convicts from prison to hospital.

Before an order could be made, the court would have to receive written or oral evidence that arrangements had been made for the offender's admission to hospital. In the existing legislation the court must be 'satisfied that arrangements had been made for the admission of the offender to hospital'. Currently, a restriction order can be made under section 65 if it is considered 'necessary for the protection of the public'. The Amendment Bill suggests this be changed to 'the protection of the public from serious harm'.

The problem of restricted patients' rights of review has not been tackled in the Bill, despite a recent critical judgment in the European Court of Human Rights. The White Paper accompanying the Bill explains that this is because the government has not had enough time to study the judgment.

I shall further discuss the Mental Health (Amendment) Bill's proposals on offenders in chapters 12 and 13.

7 Diminished Responsibility, Fitness to be Tried and Fitness to Plead

The Mental Health Act of 1959 empowers the courts to deal with mentally ill offenders by committing them to hospital and also allows for the transfer of convicted individuals from prison to hospital, as we have seen in chapter 6. But this in no way restricts the courts in their dealings with mentally ill people who commit crimes. Offenders can be placed under a probation order with a condition of psychiatric treatment (as an inpatient or outpatient), sent to prison, or, under certain circumstances, be dealt with under the legislation I am about to describe.

Diminished responsibility

The term 'diminished responsibility' is used rather loosely, often appearing in medical reports on people who may be dealt with under section 60 or section 60/65 of the Mental Health Act. Such a usage is rather a statement of opinion than a precise expression with legal significance. In legal terms the defence of diminished responsibility applies only to an indictment alleging murder; no other criminal charge can be defended in this way.

The concept of diminished responsibility was introduced in the Homicide Act of 1957, which defined capital murder and preserved capital punishment. A murder charge carried the threat of a death penalty, but if diminished responsibility was established the charge was reduced to that of manslaughter, a lesser offence not subject to so severe a punishment. Thus the legislation provided for those people charged with murder who may have been suffering at the time from some mental abnormality, and specified a less harsh punishment for such cases. If the trial judge accepted that there was diminished responsibility he could impose a sentence ranging from life imprisonment to one which did not involve either immediate or suspended custody. There have been examples of this whole range of sentencing in the past.

The following sections of the Act clarify what was intended. Section 2 (i) provides that:

> where a person kills or is the party to the killing of another, he shall not be convicted of murder if he was suffering from such abnormality of mind (whether arising from a condition of arrested or retarded development of mind or any inherent causes or induced by disease or injury) as substantially impaired his responsibility for his acts and omissions in doing or being a party to the killing.

Section 2 (ii) provides that:

> on a charge of murder it shall be for the defence to prove that the person charged is by virtue of this section not liable to be convicted of murder.

Section 2 (iii) provides that:

> a person who but for this section would be liable whether as principal or accessory to be convicted of murder shall be liable instead to be convicted of manslaughter.

Section 2 (iv) provides that:

> the fact that one party to a killing is by virtue of this section not liable to be convicted of murder shall not affect the question whether the killing amounted to murder in the case of any other party to it.

Two terms in the Act require definition: 'abnormality of mind' and 'substantially impaired'. There is much debate about these terms, and in general cases tend to be judged according to their merits. However, the ruling of Lord Parker in the case of *R*. v. *Byrne* in 1960 does throw some light on the subject. He said:

> 'abnormality of mind', which has to be contrasted with the time honoured expression of the McNaghten Rules, 'defects of reason', means a state of mind so different from that of ordinary human beings that the reasonable man would deem it abnormal. It appears to us to be wide enough to cover the mind's activities in all its aspects, not only of the perception of physical acts and matters and the ability to form a rational judgement, whether for example

the act is right or wrong, but also the ability to exercise willpower to control physical acts in accordance with that rational judgement.

In most cases the question of diminished responsibility would have been settled prior to the hearing, the decision being based on psychiatric reports obtained by both prosecution and defence. If both sides agree that there was diminished responsibility, the charge is reduced to manslaughter and the court then has to decide only upon what punishment, if any, should be given.

The following example illustrates the operation of this defence.

Some years ago Peter Baker was sentenced to two years' imprisonment for the manslaughter of his wife. The original charge had been murder, but was reduced to manslaughter by agreement between the defence and the prosecution.

Peter and June had got married in the spring of 1975 after an engagement of a year or so. He was twenty-one, she was eighteen. At first they lived with Peter's parents, but later they were able to buy a house of their own. Before their marriage they had got on well together, developing a satisfactory sexual relationship, but almost immediately after the wedding June changed, becoming greedy and demanding, both materially and sexually. She wanted an instant home full of elegant furniture, and since this was impossible she started to taunt Peter about his inadequacies as a provider. They were both working: he as a coach driver, she as a secretary. She continued by taunting him about his sexual capacity, often hinting that other men were interested in her. At times she let him prepare his own meal and then threw it away before he could eat it. They separated several times but Peter always wanted her back, despite her behaviour. He became anxious and distressed by her attitudes, and, possibly as a result, impotent. He discovered that small quantities of alcohol made him potent again, but then he began to drink more heavily, which naturally had the opposite effect.

In the spring of the following year, when June had left him once again, Peter took an overdose of pills and was admitted to hospital. June saw him there and promised that when he left they would get together again and try to start afresh. Believing her, he discharged himself, but when he met her again she told him she did not really want to go back to him, and had only said she would because he was in hospital and she didn't want to feel guilty about it. Peter became more upset but continued to meet her, the last time being a few weeks after his overdose. They went for a ride together in his car, their dog with them. After they had taken the dog for a walk, June discovered that Peter had spent some of their savings, and was furious. She swore at him, hit him, and said she would never live with him again. She called him a bastard and screamed 'I hate you, I hate you', as she pummelled his chest. Whilst she was screaming Peter put the dog-lead around her neck and strangled her. Later he went to the local police station and said he thought he had killed his wife.

There was a conflict of psychiatric opinion in this case: two psychiatrists claimed he was fully responsible, though perhaps suffering from psychopathy or immaturity, while a third considered there was a substantial impairment of responsibility. This view was in fact accepted by both the prosecution and the defence.

As this case suggests, the question of diminished responsibility is definitely a moot point where there may be a conflict of psychiatric opinions. However, the court has the final say, and experience suggests that a common-sense approach usually ensures that diminished responsibility is properly identified. Some people might claim that diminished responsibility could be used as an excuse for almost any act of murder, but in practice the law does not work in this way, and while it is sometimes in error, it tends on the whole to arrive at the right decision. It is sentencing that presents the greatest problems. In two cases similar to the one above, one offender received a life sentence while another was placed on probation. Peter Baker's sentence fell between these extremes.

Fitness to be tried and fitness to plead

When someone is arrested because of possible involvement in a crime, it may be discovered that he is mentally ill. At this stage the police may decide that he should be dealt with by the psychiatric services — either as an informal patient, or, more usually, under part 4 of the Mental Health Act 1959. This is only likely to happen if the individual is suspected of a minor offence, such as vagrancy or behaviour likely to lead to a breach of the peace. If a more serious crime is suspected he will be charged and any decision about his future left to the courts.

It may be found that the man is suffering from a severe

mental illness, raising questions of his fitness to be tried and fitness to plead. These are questions quite separate from the raising of a defence of insanity at trial.

Fitness to be tried

The question of fitness to be tried is different from that of fitness to plead: the accused must be brought to trial before a decision can be made on his fitness to plead, but it may be considered ill-advised to bring him to trial at all, and this is what concerns fitness to be tried.

The Criminal Lunatics Act 1884 allows the Home Secretary to exercise his power 'where the prisoner's condition is such that the immediate removal to a mental hospital is necessary, that it would not be practicable to bring him before a Court, or that the trial is likely to have an injurious effect on his mental state'. It goes on to state that 'the issue of insanity should be determined by the jury whenever possible and the power should be exercised only when there is likely to be a scandal if the prisoner is brought for trial'. The law on this matter is also set out in section 73 of the Mental Health Act 1959:

> If in the case of a person to whom this section applies the Secretary of State is satisfied by the like reports as are required for the last foregoing section that that person is suffering from mental illness or severe subnormality of a nature or degree which warrants the detention of the patient in a hospital for medical treatment, the Secretary of State shall have the like power of giving a transfer direction in respect of him under that section as if he were serving a sentence of imprisonment.

Here we are clearly concerned with the person who has not yet been dealt with by the court. Before exercising his powers under either section the Home Secretary must be satisfied by reports from a minimum of two medical practitioners, at least one of whom must be a practitioner approved by the Secretary of State as having special experience in the diagnosis or treatment of mental disorders for the purposes of section 28 of the Mental Health Act 1959.

Section 73 applies to:

(a) persons committed in custody for trial at the Crown Court or committed in custody to the Crown Court under section 6 or section 8 of the Criminal Justice Act 1948 and persons in custody pending a retrial ordered under section 7 of the Criminal Appeal Act 1968;

(b) persons committed in custody to the Crown Court under section 28 or section 29 of the Magistrates' Courts Act 1952, section 5 of the Vagrancy Act 1824, or section 67 of this Act;

(c) persons remanded in custody by the Crown Court to await a judgement or sentence which has been respited;

(d) persons remanded in custody by a magistrates' court;

(e) civil prisoners, that is to say persons committed by a court to prison for a limited term (including persons committed to prison in pursuance of a writ of attachment), not being persons failing to be dealt with under section 72 of this Act;

(f) aliens detained in a prison or other institution to which the Prison Act 1952 applies, in pursuance of the Aliens Order 1953, or any order amending or replacing that order.

Fitness to plead

When a defendant is brought up for trial he or she may be found to be unfit to plead to the indictment under section 4 of the Criminal Procedure (Insanity) Act 1964. Though the Act sets down the provision, the courts themselves have evolved over the years the criteria for judging whether a defendant is under a disability that makes him unfit to plead. The tests seem to be: is the defendant able to understand the charge? is he able to understand the difference between pleas of guilty and not guilty? is he able to challenge jurors? is he able to instruct counsel? is he able to follow the evidence? If he is capable of all these things he has a right to be tried if he so wishes, even if he is not capable of acting in his own best interests.

Once again it is usual for the court to receive medical evidence, and the question of fitness to plead is determined by a jury empanelled for this purpose. Although in most cases the issue will be raised before arraignment, section 4(2) of the Criminal Procedure (Insanity) Act 1964 provides that the court, if it feels it expedient to do so, may postpone the question of fitness to plead until the opening of the case for the defence. An example where such a course would be proper is where there is a reasonable chance that the evidence for the prosecution will be successfully challenged, so that the defence is not called upon.

In deciding whether it is expedient to try the issue of fitness to plead prior to arraignment, the judge should first assess the strength of the prosecution case as disclosed in the committal documents and then consider the nature and degree of the supposed disability as revealed by any medical reports or evidence before him. He then has to decide whether it is expedient and in the defendant's interests to postpone the trial of the issue of fitness to plead, so affording him the opportunity of an acquittal, or whether it is expedient to try the issue of fitness to plead before arraignment.

The following example shows how someone who is unfit to plead may be tried to his advantage.

Mr Ralph Edwards was charged on six counts relating to two separate offences. One offence was taking and driving away a vehicle without the owner's consent and the theft of the vehicle's contents. The second was the burglary of a house, attempted murder of the occupant, wounding with intent and assault with intent to rob. Mr Edwards at first pleaded guilty to both offences, but later denied the second charge completely. He had a past history of schizophrenia and his solicitors thought he was possibly unfit to plead. He was examined while on remand by a psychiatrist who had treated him in the past, and found to be withdrawn and depressed. There was also evidence of thought disorder, ideas of reference (believing that others were referring to him by their words and gestures) and passivity (a feeling of being under some outside control). He also described several vague paranoid delusions. He admitted to stealing the motor vehicle and disposing of its contents, but firmly denied the other more serious charges. He claimed he had confessed to them initially because 'nothing mattered'. He wanted to go to prison and thought it would gain him revenge on his mother, who had apparently informed the police of his first offence. He said that he did not wish to put up any defence and wanted to be dealt with by the court as quickly and as severely as possible.

The evidence on the second charge was not convincing, but Mr Edwards was obviously unable to instruct a solicitor satisfactorily and would have to be considered unfit to plead. The possibility of treatment before the trial was explored, and his counsel asked for him to be admitted to hospital on bail; this the court allowed.

In the past Mr Edwards had usually responded well to treatment, a pattern repeated on this occasion, when he recovered sufficiently to instruct his legal advisors and was finally tried. He was found guilty of the first group of offences, but not guilty of the second. He was dealt with under section 60 of the Mental Health Act and readmitted to hospital. The judge made it clear that he did not consider the accused to be in any way a violent person.

The case below provides an example of someone unfit to plead who has little chance of ever becoming fit to plead.

Jimmy Crewe was a normal child until he was involved in an accident at the age of ten. He was knocked down by a car when crossing the road, and sustained a severe head injury. He was admitted to hospital, where it was thought he was likely to die, but he did recover, though from that point his intellectual ability was severely retarded and he suffered from uncontrolled outbursts of temper. When he was fourteen he attacked his mother with a hatchet, lacerating her scalp. She told no one, saying when she went for hospital treatment that she had fallen off a stool and cut her head on a metal fender. Jimmy continued to have violent outbursts; when he was eighteen he attacked a neighbour, knocking him unconscious with an iron bar. This time the police were involved and he was arrested, following which it became obvious that he was severely mentally handicapped. His vocabulary was limited and he appeared completely unconcerned about what he had done and about his present position. He appeared in the Magistrates' Court and was remanded in custody for psychiatric reports. The magistrates judged that he was unfit to plead and when he was seen by a solicitor who had been asked to take charge of the case by Jimmy's parents, it was found that he had no comprehension that he was charged with attempted murder, appeared not to know the meaning of the word guilty, and could give no explanation of what he had done, or why.

The prison medical officer and a psychiatrist, called in to give their opinion, agreed that he was suffering from a severe degree of mental handicap making him unfit to plead. When he appeared in the Crown Court, the jury found him unfit to plead and he was committed to a special hospital.

The court has powers to postpone trial in order that the individual can be treated and perhaps make sufficient improvement to become fit to plead. Every effort should be made to hold a trial if at all possible, since being unfit to plead leaves doubts whether the individual did in fact commit an offence. Many serious mental illnesses can be improved by treatment, but there are others, in particular severe mental handicap, where treatment is rarely very effective, and in these cases there seems to be no point in deferring the trial.

' Rights

It is easy to think of mental patients as people apart from the rest of us. We may have feelings of compassion toward them, but we often fail to recognize that their problems, rights and difficulties could be ours. No one is immune to mental disorder, nor to being regarded as abnormal by others. For these reasons the rights of mental patients should be the concern of us all.

Since any of us might be suspected of being mentally ill at some time in our lives, it is worth examining what rights the individual has to resist being dragged into the psychiatric net. A whole range of people can decide that an individual is mentally ill, and some of them are empowered to act on their belief. Your family, friends, employer, neighbours, or anyone else who is in contact with you may come to believe that you are ill, and may notify your doctor or your local social services department, who in turn may ignore or act upon this information. Your family doctor or a social worker may ask to see you or visit you, but they can do little without your consent unless they employ the powers set down in part 4 of the Mental Health Act. If there is something genuinely wrong you may indeed welcome their offer of help, or be persuaded to accept help from elsewhere; you may then be treated as an outpatient or a day patient, or admitted to hospital. (The possible courses of action once you have been admitted to hospital will be considered later.)

At this stage, if you deny there is anything wrong and refuse treatment you should be left alone unless it is considered that there are grounds for compulsory admission to hospital. If so you have little power to resist at this stage. Under section 29 of the Act your family doctor can compulsorily admit you to hospital, where you can be detained for three days. The family doctor may seek the help of a consultant psychiatrist; you may then be admitted to hospital under section 25 of the Act and detained there for a maximum of one month. In neither of these cases can you appeal, or even attempt legally to prevent your admission or detention. There is one exception: theoretically it is possible to use the law on habeas corpus, but this is much more a potential than a practical safeguard.

The Amendment Bill proposes that patients detained under section 25 should be allowed to apply to a Mental Health Review Tribunal within fourteen days from the date they are admitted to hospital.

The powers provided under section 26 of the Act can also be used, but these require consent of the nearest relative, which may be withheld. In this event a case must be made for removing the rights of the nearest relative and taking the matter before a magistrate. Another example of compulsory admittance might occur if you happen to be in a public place, when a constable is able, as we have seen, to remove you to 'a place of safety' using the powers provided by section 136.

From these instances it can be seen that any member of the public can be compulsorily admitted to a mental hospital or psychiatric unit. The only real safeguard against this happening improperly is the integrity of social workers, the medical profession and the police force.

In hospital
There is a common belief that informal patients in psychiatric units, hospitals or registered nursing homes are in exactly the same position as patients with 'physical' diseases in general hospitals. This is not actually true, since psychiatric patients, whether compulsorily or informally admitted, lose certain rights that people outside hospital accept as their due. For instance, section 36 of the Act allows the responsible medical officer to withhold correspondence if he considers it could interfere with the treatment of the patient or cause unnecessary distress. The responsible medical officer can prevent the patient sending letters or parcels to people who have notified the hospital managers or himself in writing that they do not want to receive communications from the patient. He can also intercept any correspondence which he believes is unreasonably offensive to the addressee, likely to prejudice the interest of the patient, or defamatory to other people, excepting members of the hospital staff.

This section of the Act states specifically that letters are exempt from interception if addressed to certain individuals and bodies, namely: the Secretary of State for Health; any member of Parliament; the master, deputy master, or any other officer of the Court of Protection; the managers of the hospital; any person or authority having powers to discharge the patient under part 4 of the Act; and the Mental Health Review Tribunal, provided the patient is entitled to make application to it. Section 134 states that section 36 of the Act applies to informal patients as well as to patients detained compulsorily. In guardianship orders the same restriction on correspondence can be made, except that here the guardian has the same powers as the responsible medical officer or the managers of the hospital.

The Amendment Bill would ensure that informal patients could send and receive correspondence without interference; interception would be limited to cases where patients detained in special hospitals sent postal packets to people who had specifically stated in writing that they did not wish to receive them. In these cases patients would have to be informed within twenty-four hours that their packages had been withheld.

Postal packets could not be intercepted under any circumstances if addressed to: any Minister of the Crown or member of either House of Parliament; the master, deputy master, or any other officer of the Court of Protection, or any of the Lord Chancellor's visitors; the Parliamentary Commissioner for Administration; the Health Service Commissioner for England; the Health Service Commissioner for Wales; a local commissioner within the meaning of part 3 of the Local Government Act of 1974, a Mental Health Review Tribunal; a Health Authority within the meaning of the National Health Service Act 1977; a Local Social Service Authority; a Community Health Council; a Probation and After-Care Committee appointed under paragraph 2 of schedule 3 of the Powers of Criminal Courts Act 1973; the managers of the hospital in which the patient is detained; any legally qualified person instructed by the patient to act as his legal adviser; the European Commission for Human Rights, or the European Court of Human Rights.

Informal patients can, as we have seen, be detained compulsorily in the hospital if the responsible medical officer considers this to be necessary; this can be achieved initially under section 30 of the Act, followed by detention under section 25 or 26 if considered appropriate. Informal patients cannot be forced to have treatment in hospital, while compulsorily detained patients can. However, the legislation is open to interpretation, and it can be argued that no powers exist to oblige patients detained compulsorily to accept the treatment prescribed. Even so, some people consider that the Act does imply such powers, and in practice it does happen that patients are given treatment against their wishes.

The Amendment Bill confronts this problem and proposes that general medical and nursing care, including rehabilitation, could be provided without the detained patient's permission. In the case of treatments that are 'hazardous, irreversible or not fully established', not only must the patient give his consent, but an independent doctor must also agree that the treatment is necessary. For other treatments, including the administration of medicines, either the patient must give his consent, or, if he refuses, an independent doctor must certify that the treatment is necessary and desirable.

Thus the concept of a second opinion has been introduced; this goes some way towards satisfying many people's anxieties. However, it has been suggested that a multi-disciplinary panel, rather than an independent doctor, should make the decision as to whether treatment is necessary.

An exception to these conditions is made in the case of 'emergencies'. To quote the Bill, the conditions would not apply to any treatment:

(a) which is immediately necessary to save the patient's life: or
(b) which (not being irreversible) is immediately necessary to prevent a serious deterioration of his condition: or
(c) which (not being irreversible or hazardous) represents the minimal interference necessary to prevent the patient from behaving violently, or being a danger to himself, or others.

The situation concerning voting rights is equally confused. On the whole, patients who have a home address and are on the electoral register are allowed to vote, while patients whose only address is a psychiatric hospital are denied this right, despite a ruling to the contrary. Because of the ambiguity of the legal position, patients in psychiatric units of general hospitals can use the hospital address and vote, even though this would probably not be possible were their address that of a mental hospital. A recent judge's ruling suggests that large numbers of mental hospital patients can and should be allowed to vote. He was considering the case of some patients in a hospital for the mentally handicapped; they were considered by the responsible medical officer to be no longer suffering from any mental disorder, and only remained because of their physical disabilities. The ruling suggests that psychiatrists will be able to decide whether their patients should have the vote – an extremely unsatisfactory situation.

Patients compulsorily detained in hospital or taken into guardianship can appeal by making an application to a Mental Health Review Tribunal. Those detained under sections 29, 25, or 72 of the Act do not enjoy this right, though those whose discharge is restricted under sections 65 and 74 of the Act may register an appeal. The Mental Health Review Tribunal cannot then actually order a patient's discharge; it is only empowered to recommend it to the Home Secretary.

As I have already mentioned, the Amendment Bill would allow patients detained under section 25 to apply to a Mental Health Review Tribunal.

Mental Health Review Tribunals

A patient who is admitted to hospital under an order for treatment may apply to a Mental Health Review Tribunal within a period of six months from the day of admission or from his or her sixteenth birthday, whichever is the later. The same rules apply to a patient received into guardianship.

People detained under section 60 of the Act have the same rights to appeal to a Mental Health Tribunal as those detained under section 26 or under a guardianship order. If a restriction on discharge is placed on the patient under section 65 or 74 of the Act, an application can still be made to a Mental Health Review Tribunal, but it may not order discharge even if considered advisable; it can only make recommendations to the Home Secretary.

An application to a Mental Health Review Tribunal must be made in writing and addressed to the tribunal for the appropriate area: that containing the hospital where the patient is detained, or that in which the patient is residing, in the case of guardianship. Each Regional Health Authority has its own Mental Health Review Tribunal. A tribunal is composed of three people: a legal member, a medical member and one other person with experience in administration or social services, or with some other qualifications or expertise that may be considered suitable. The members of the tribunal are appointed by the Lord Chancellor, who consults with the Secretary of State for Health on the selection of the latter two members. The legal member always acts as the chairman.

Mental Health Review Tribunals may meet in public or in private. The Lord Chancellor has power to rule on this matter as on others concerning the functioning of the tribunal. A tribunal may consider an application without a formal hearing if it is believed such a hearing would be detrimental to the health of the patient, or if the applicant wishes the application to be dealt with informally. An applicant may be seen by one or more members of the tribunal before the hearing, and it is usual for the medical member to see the patient in this way. The applicant can be represented by a friend, but may not have legal representation in the normal sense, though the 'friend' may be a solicitor or barrister.

Before a tribunal the responsible medical officer prepares a report; these may also be obtained from other sources, including the nursing staff and the hospital social worker, or a community worker who is able to contribute to the decision making of the tribunal. For example, arrangements may be made to accommodate the patient if he or she is discharged from the hospital, and the relevant information can be presented to the tribunal in a report. Proper preparation for the tribunal can generally only be achieved if the patient has adequate help from some individual or organization concerned about his or her welfare. As a rule the patient applies to the tribunal and later appears before it unsupported and unprepared. He or she is entitled to see all the documents presented to the tribunal unless it is considered that they would be harmful to his or her mental health or future treatment. This means that the responsible medical officer's report can be withheld, or withheld in part, from the patient.

A Mental Health Review Tribunal may reject the application or order the patient's release. It is not empowered to do anything else except make recommendations; it cannot order the transfer of a patient from one hospital to another, or make any rulings about his or her future care, other than permitting discharge from the compulsory order under which he or she has been detained. A tribunal can refer a case to the High Court if there is any point of law involved; under certain circumstances it may be requested by the High Court to make such a referral.

It is significant that the Act specifically states that the Arbitration Act 1950 shall not apply to any proceedings before a Mental Health Review Tribunal, except so far as any provision of that Act may be applied, with or without modification, by rules made under section 124 of the Act. Section 124 covers the rules of procedure for a Mental Health Review Tribunal.

It can be seen that Mental Health Review Tribunals are capable of protecting patients from unnecessary or improper detention in psychiatric establishments, but they do not protect people admitted compulsorily for short periods under sections 25 and 29 of the Act, and their structure and procedures are such as to load the dice rather heavily in favour of the hospital and against the patient. Expert witnesses can be called to give evidence to the tribunal in support of detaining the patient, who may in contrast be left to present his or her own case without outside help, unless some individual or organization happens to take an interest and assists in the preparation of the case and its presentation before the tribunal. Studies have shown that many more patients are granted release from hospital by Mental Health Review Tribunals when they are helped and represented than when they receive no assistance. This part of the Act should be changed to give every patient who applies to a Mental Health Review Tribunal the right to help in preparing a case and in representation at the tribunal.

The Mental Health (Amendment) Bill would not only allow patients detained under section 25 of the principal Act to apply to Mental Health Review Tribunals, but would also make it obligatory for the hospital managers to refer detained patients' cases to a Mental Health Review Tribunal if patients had not made an application, or if they had made an application but withdrawn it. These applications would be made when the period for application expired.

The Bill would also allow patients under the age of 16 to apply to a Mental Health Review Tribunal. Other changes proposed in the Bill concern the concept of treatability and the alleviation, or prevention of deterioration, of the patient's condition. These suggestions are consistent with the changes made in the compulsory orders, such as section 26.

The Amendment Bill also proposes that any medical practitioner authorized by, or on behalf of, the patient should be able at any reasonable time to visit and examine the patient in private, and be entitled to inspect any records relating to the patient's treatment in any hospital. This is usually allowed at present but is not mentioned in the principal Act.

Protection of staff

Section 141 of the Act protects staff from frivolous litigation; in doing so it denies all patients in psychiatric establishments a basic right. A patient cannot take a civil action or institute criminal proceedings against a member of staff of a hospital without leave of the High Court, and, to quote the Act, 'the High Court shall not give leave under this Section unless satisfied that there is substantial ground for the contention that the person to be proceeded against has acted in bad faith, or without reasonable care'. Thus, if a patient is assaulted by a member of staff, neither criminal nor civil proceedings can be taken without prior leave from the High Court, which can easily refuse to grant it, given the wording of the Act as quoted above. 'Substantial grounds' can be interpreted to mean that the evidence against the member of staff must be overwhelming, much more convincing than would be the case in a normal criminal or civil action. A similar, equally unsatisfactory situation exists in the prison service. Clearly, it is possible that patients and prisoners might make unjustified complaints against members of staff, but this is equally true of the general public. Surely it is unjust to discriminate between those people who have been labelled mentally ill and the rest of us when an individual has been the victim of assault, abuse or other malpractice and wishes to take legal action?

Simply to label someone as mentally ill causes that person to lose certain rights normally regarded as natural and inviolable in our society. It may be argued that victims of mental illness are entitled to extra rights, such as the rights to be treated and to have adequate community help and support, and it may even be claimed that these rights exist in reality, but they are certainly not legal rights. Most therapeutic provision, community help and support of the mentally ill do not exist by right; moreover, they are often inadequate, patchily distributed and ineffective. The Mental Health Act of 1959 empowers certain authorities to detain people compulsorily in institutions and to restrict their rights to those of a child younger than sixteen, yet nothing in the Act forces either the Health Service or local authority social services departments to provide the kind of treatment and help that might obviate the need for compulsory detention and even admission to hospital.

The development of psychiatric services in some parts of the United Kingdom has shown how most patients can be treated, helped and supported without admission to hospital or recourse to legal force. But unfortunately nothing obliges hospitals and local authorities to establish such regimes, and hence those that do not can fall back on custodial care and lavish use of compulsion. In some areas patients are not accepted by hospitals in the evenings or at weekends unless they are the subjects of a compulsory order, regardless of their own wishes about entering hospital. Compulsory powers are also used to enforce the transfer of patients from one hospital to another if they raise objections. For example, a woman might be seen in the accident and emergency department of a general hospital and accept the fact that she needs inpatient treatment. She might agree to go to a local general hospital psychiatric unit, but if it is decided that she should go to a mental hospital instead, and she refuses, a compulsory order might be used. This is not because the patient has refused to enter hospital, but because the doctor or authority concerned has decided she should go to a specific hospital for purely administrative reasons. In at least one district, where it was difficult to obtain a psychiatric opinion quickly, patients who were seen in the accident and emergency department and thought to need psychiatric treatment were compulsorily admitted to the local psychiatric unit if they refused to go there informally. In many of these cases people needed not inpatient treatment but psychiatric advice.

Compulsory powers for admitting people to hospital are necessary for protecting them against themselves and for safeguarding orders; equally there is a need for legislation that manages the affairs of people who are unable to cope for themselves. But such powers, once available, can easily be abused, and there is an urgent need to devise safeguards against potential abuses of the laws on compulsory admission, treatment and control of patients' affairs.

The Mental Health (Amendment) Bill provides for the establishment of a Mental Health Act Commission, similar in some ways to the Scottish Mental Welfare Commission (see chapter 10). Its members would include lawyers, doctors, nurses, psychologists, social workers and laymen, and it would have a number of responsibilities, including checking on patients' detention, visiting psychiatric hospitals (including the special hospitals) and appointing independent doctors to give opinions on whether treatment should be administered against patients' wishes. The Commission would also be responsible for specifying the treatments that give rise to special concern and for the drawing up of a code of practice.

9 Control of your Own Affairs

Most people who develop mental illnesses do not lose any civil rights and are capable of looking after their own affairs. Even serious mental illness does not in itself interfere with people's ability to manage their lives. It is important to emphasize this, since many people have exaggerated notions of mental illness and believe that its victims are incapable even of caring for themselves, let alone managing financial matters and coping with all the other complications of normal life. However, there are a few mentally ill and mentally handi-capped people who do need help in managing their affairs, and this can be provided in two ways, by the use of power of attorney and by the involvement of the Court of Protection.

Power of attorney
Any adult can grant power of attorney to someone else, who is then able to act on his or her behalf in dealing with finances and other matters. The criteria for power of attorney are rather similar to those for testamentary capacity, as we shall see. The person giving power of attorney must know what the act means and appreciate its consequences, and should not be abnormally suggestible. There are a number of ways of testing for suggestibility: one might, for instance, ask a man for a charity donation and see if he is prepared to hand it over without asking any questions or hesitating to think the matter over.

On the whole the use of power of attorney is limited; most people who are able to give it are not in need of protection, and will only tend to make use of the provision if they are unable to get out and about to deal with their affairs — because they are in hospital, for example. Some elderly people give power of attorney because they wish to be rid of the harrass-ment of bills, rates, income tax and the other irritating paraphernalia of modern life. In deciding on the use of power of attorney it is essential to find out as much as possible about the person nominated to act for the patient, and to obtain a medical opinion as to the patient's ability and understanding.

Having mentioned testamentary capacity, I shall now look at this topic before going on to the second way of helping people to deal with their affairs.

Testamentary capacity
The presence of a mental illness does not prevent someone from making a contract or a will. It is essential, however, that the person understands the process and what it involves. Testamentary capacity requires that the individual:
(1) understand the nature and extent of his property;
(2) be aware of the persons who have claims upon his bounty;
(3) possess judgement and will sufficiently unclouded and free as to enable him to determine the relative strength of these claims;
(4) not be abnormally suggestible or under the influence of drugs or alcohol.

Someone may well be depressed, with a sense of unworthiness, or a victim of schizophrenia, with delusions of persecution, and yet be able, in legal terms, to enter into a contract or make a will. On the other hand, someone who had developed delusional beliefs about her children would not be of testamentary capacity even if her reasoning was unimpaired in other ways. A man who was fully aware of his property and possessions and knew exactly who had claims upon his bounty but who was abnormally suggestible, could not be considered of testamentary capacity, since anyone assisting with the making of the will might be able to sway his judgement and ensure that he or she became a beneficiary.

The following cases illustrate the sort of problems that may arise.

Mrs Williams was a lady of seventy-five: a rather suspicious individual all her life, with a tendency to blame others if anything went wrong. Since she was seventy-three her memory had been gradually failing, so that she tended to misplace things at home and forget that she had paid for food or settled bills. As a result of these memory lapses she grew to believe that her daughter, who lived nearby, was interfering with her belongings and stealing her money. Her daughter was caring and sympathetic. She managed to cope with her mother's accusations, helped by counselling from her doctor. The old lady had made a will in favour of her three children, but decided to change it so as to exclude this daughter.

Careful assessment of Mrs Williams and an examination of her family situation showed that she was not now of testamentary capacity, and so she was unable to change her will.

Mr Lee developed a depressive illness when he was forty-five. He made a good recovery with treatment, but had a number of relapses during the next ten years. In his late fifties he again became depressed; this attack was prolonged and resistant to treatment. During this period, while in hospital, he decided that it was time to make a will. An examination was carried out in order to determine his testamentary capacity. He was fully aware of his possessions and who had claims on them, but expressed a wish to leave all his money to the hospital. During his examination it was suggested that he could, if he so wished, hand over all his money before his death; agreeing, he asked if he could sign a document to this effect. He was considered abnormally suggestible and therefore not of testamentary capacity, and so he did not make a will. Later, after a gradual recovery, he did actually make a will leaving a small sum to the hospital but including appropriate bequests to his family.

The Court of Protection

When someone who is suffering from a mental disorder becomes incapable of managing his or her own affairs, the usual procedure is to apply to the Court of Protection for an order appointing a receiver. The Court of Protection is an office of the Supreme Court of Judicature and operates under the direction of a master nominated by the Lord Chancellor and assisted by a deputy and assistant masters.

Section 101 of the Mental Health Act 1959 gives the court jurisdiction when medical evidence shows that a person is incapable of managing his or her affairs by reason of mental disorder. To recap, mental disorder is defined in section 4 paragraph 1 of the Act as 'mental illness, arrested or incomplete development of mind, psychopathic disorder and any other disorder or disability of mind'. Section 4 paragraph 4 of the Act defines 'psychopathic disorder' as 'a permanent disorder or disability of mind (whether or not including subnormality of intelligence) which results in abnormally aggressive or seriously irresponsible conduct on the part of the patient and requires or is susceptible to medical treatment'. The court's jurisdiction extends to the estates of minors, but it is not exercised if the estate is already adequately protected by other means, such as the appointment of trustees.

An application to the court for the appointment of a receiver is normally made by the nearest relative of the patient. In the case of small estates, the relative may apply through the personal application branch of the court without seeking any legal assistance. When the estate is large it is usual to consult a solicitor. If the nearest relative is unable or unwilling to apply, another relative or friend of the patient may do so, but here the reasons for the application should be clearly stated. Where there is no relative or friend, a solicitor or a creditor of the patient may make an application. Sometimes an officer of a local authority may be authorized to apply by his or her council. If no one is willing, a solicitor should report this to the court; directions may then be given for one of the officers of the court or the official solicitor of the Supreme Court of Judicature to apply. Here as elsewhere medical evidence must be obtained, but if this is difficult the court is empowered to send a Lord Chancellor's visitor to the patient's home to prepare a report for the court.

Depending upon the value of the patient's estate, certificate forms or affidavit forms are necessary. Affidavit forms must be used if the value of the patient's estate exceeds £3,000 and his income exceeds £300 a year. For lower amounts, certificate forms are required. Printed forms for use in the proceedings are obtainable free of charge from the Court Office, 25 Store Street, London WC1E 7BP, or from the Form Room, Royal Courts of Justice, London WC2A 2LL. Three forms need to be sent to the court:

(1) The application form (CP1) in duplicate.
(2) An affidavit of kindred and fortune, form CP4, or a certificate of kindred and fortune, form CP5.
(3) A medical certificate on form CP3.

The forms are self-explanatory. The one covering kindred and fortune asks about the individual's money, property, liabilities and so on, while the medical certificate asks for a diagnosis supported by evidence, and an explanation of why the individual is unable to manage his or her own affairs. (In the past medical affidavits were sometimes necessary, but now medical certificates are sufficient.)

It is not usually necessary for anyone to attend the hearing of the application, but the master may in special circumstances ask for the solicitor to attend, and, on rare occasions, the applicant or other people involved. Following the hearing a receiver is appointed. The preference of the court is to appoint the nearest relative as receiver, which has certain disadvantages, as I shall explain. However, if good reasons are presented to the court stating why the nearest relative should not be appointed, someone else may be chosen – another relative, or a friend. A solicitor, accountant or land agent may be appointed as receiver. Sometimes an officer of a local authority may be appointed, though this generally only happens in cases concerning people who are resident in local authority homes. When there is no suitable person, or when there is family friction, the official solicitor may be appointed as receiver. It is unusual to appoint someone who is not resident in the United Kingdom as a receiver.

Before the hearing the patient must be served with a notice on form CP6 and the person serving the notice must swear an affidavit to this effect (form CP7). If a medical practitioner serves the notice, a certificate of service on form CP7 should be filed instead of an affidavit.

In most cases, the receiver has to give security for the money passing through his or her hands, and generally for all acts as receiver. The amount is fixed on the hearing of the application and notified to the solicitor. Security can take the form of a fidelity guarantee bond, or lodgement of cash or investments in court. The receiver is expected to present accounts yearly or two-yearly. This may be done in person or by way of a solicitor.

If the court does not agree that a receiver should be appointed, the applicant may seek an appointment with the master to reopen the matter. For this purpose a summons should be issued. On the hearing of the summons the master may confirm or revoke his previous order or decision, or take any other action he thinks fit. Any person aggrieved by an order or decision of the master can serve notice of appeal, which must be lodged within eight days of the decision. Appeals can be made to the Court of Appeal and thence to the House of Lords.

If the patient later improves and becomes able to manage his own affairs, he can make an application, supported by a medical certificate, to resume his normal responsibilities. The court may grant this request or reject it. If the master has doubts about the medical evidence, he may request one of the Lord Chancellor's visitors to see the patient and prepare a report. These may be either medical or legal visitors appointed by the Lord Chancellor. They are called upon to visit patients whose affairs may need to be handled by the Court of Protection or have already been dealt with by the appointment of a receiver.

As we have seen, the Court of Protection tends, unless there is a specific objection, to appoint the nearest relative as receiver. In most cases this is an appropriate choice, but sometimes not — he or she might not have the patient's best interest at heart and might even benefit from restricting the amount of money the patient is allowed to have. The following examples illustrate the kind of case where receivership is necessary and some of the disadvantages of appointing the nearest relative as receiver.

Mrs Ellis lived in a large, elegantly furnished house that she had found difficult to manage since the death of her husband some years earlier. At the age of eighty-five she began to be forgetful, and developed a tendency to go out shopping in the middle of the night. This worried her neighbours, and one of them approached her family doctor. He saw Mrs Ellis and arranged for some community support, including a home help and meals-on-wheels. He prescribed a mild sedative to be taken at night, but Mrs Ellis never bothered with it and still sallied forth to the shops at unusual hours. Her family doctor sought the advice of a psychiatrist, who arranged day care and again prescribed a mild sedative, which again was never used. However, attending hospital during the day did make Mrs Ellis tired by the evening, and she started to sleep normally again.

Sadly she had a fall about six months later, fracturing the neck of her femur. She was admitted to hospital and made a reasonable recovery, but had difficulty in walking and could no longer care for herself. She expressed a wish to return home, but was unable to make any suitable arrangements. It was decided that her affairs should be placed in the hands of a receiver and an appropriate application was made to the

Court of Protection. Her nearest relative, a niece, was appointed receiver. She advertised for a resident housekeeper and succeeded in finding one; Mrs Ellis was then able to return home and resume day hospital care. She lived for a further eighteen months, finally dying after a stroke.

Mr Joseph was an eccentric old gentleman who had never married and had spent most of his life living in various hotels. He had been involved in the diamond trade and was quite well off. At the age of seventy-five he started to develop a dementing illness, becoming forgetful and getting lost whenever he went out for a walk. He was living in a small hotel, but then developed a severe chest infection and had to be admitted to hospital. He recovered from the infection, but it became clear that he was unable to manage his own affairs. A psychiatric opinion was sought and it was decided that it would be best to appoint a receiver. After an application to the Court of Protection his younger brother was appointed. Mr Joseph's doctor thought he was well enough to move to a rest home, and appropriate accommodation was found. However, the younger brother objected, saying that he ought to remain in hospital. The doctor spent a lot of time trying to persuade the brother that a rest home would provide a better environment than the hospital, but to no avail. The doctor had a prolonged correspondence with the Court of Protection and the brother, but nothing was done. Finally the old gentleman died from a further chest infection. He had been in hospital for thirteen months.

There are large numbers of old people in long-stay geriatric wards and psychiatric hospitals who have no relatives and only a tiny income from their old age pension or other pensions, but who are not allowed to spend this money on themselves because of their mental disability. Over a period even the small sums they receive mount up and might be used to provide extra comforts, or pay for a holiday. Unfortunately this is not possible unless patients' affairs are taken over by the Court of Protection and a receiver appointed. This rarely happens because of the relatively small amounts of money involved and the problem of finding an appropriate receiver, coupled with the prospect that if all these cases were presented to the Court of Protection it would have great difficulties in coping with them. There is an urgent need to find a simple way of dealing with these cases and to establish a system where receivers are provided either by the Health Service or by local authorities.

People should always be encouraged to look after their own affairs, but when this becomes impossible the existing methods of obtaining help should be made available to them. However, these methods are not always appropriate or effective, and, as I have suggested, certain changes and reforms would bring great improvements.

10 Mental Health Legislation in Scotland

Mental health legislation in Scotland has significant differences to that in England and Wales, though there are naturally some similarities in both spirit and practice. The Mental Health (Scotland) Act 1960 governs the same subjects as the Mental Health Act 1959 in England and Wales. Before the latter Act was passed the compulsory admission of patients to psychiatric hospitals other than in cases of emergency required orders signed by magistrates. Scotland has retained this principle, with the sheriff making compulsory orders based on medical evidence. Before considering the processes involved in compulsory admission, appeal and so on, it is worth looking at some of the other differences between legislation in the two Acts.

Definitions
The Mental Health Act 1959 defines 'mental disorder', 'subnormality', 'severe subnormality' and 'psychopathic disorder'. In the Scottish Act, section 6 states: 'In this Act "mental disorder" means mental illness or mental deficiency however caused or manifested.' This is the only definition in the whole Act. Psychopathy is not mentioned and there is no differentiation between different types of subnormality (or mental handicap, as it is now called).

The England and Wales Act mentions mental welfare officers, who are now social workers designated as mental welfare officers. In the Scottish Act such social workers are referred to as mental health officers, and have similar duties and powers to their equivalents in England and Wales.

The Mental Welfare Commission
There is no Mental Welfare Commission in England and Wales, but the Mental Health (Scotland) Act 1960 set up such a body to replace the old Board of Control, or, as it was called in Scotland, the General Board of Control for Scotland.

Before the 1959 Act there was a Board of Control in England and Wales too, but it was abolished and never replaced.

Broadly speaking, the Mental Welfare Commission has the same duties and functions as the old Board of Control in England and Wales and in Scotland. It is expected to exercise a protective function over people who are incapable of taking care of themselves or their interests properly because of mental disorder, and it can discharge patients who are compulsorily detained in hospital or subject to guardianship orders.

The Mental Welfare Commission is made up of between seven and nine commissioners, including at least one woman, and headed by a chairman. At least three of the commissioners must be medical practitioners, and at least one must be a member of the Faculty of Advocates or a solicitor. The commissioners are appointed by Her Majesty the Queen, on the recommendation of the Secretary of State for Scotland.

Section 4 of the Act establishes the functions of the Mental Welfare Commission:

(a) to make enquiry into any case where it appears to them that there may be ill-treatment, deficiency in care or treatment, or improper detention of any person who may be suffering from mental disorder, or where the property of any such person may, by reason of his mental disorder, be exposed to loss or damage;

(b) to visit regularly, and as often as they may think appropriate, patients who are liable to be detained in a hospital or who are subject to guardianship, and on any such visit to afford an opportunity, on request, for private interview to any such patient as aforesaid or, where the patient is in a hospital, to any other patient in that hospital;

(c) to bring to the attention of any board of management or of any local authority the facts of any case in which in the opinion of the Mental Welfare Commission it is desirable for the board of management or the local authority to exercise any of the functions of that board or of that authority to secure the welfare of any patient suffering from mental disorder by —
   (i) preventing his ill-treatment;
   (ii) remedying any deficiency in his care or treatment;
   (iii) terminating his improper detention;
   (iv) preventing or redressing loss or damage to his property.

Admission to hospital

Part 4 of the Act covers admission to hospital, detention and guardianship. As in the England and Wales Act, there is an assumption that most patients will be admitted informally, though this subject is dealt with only briefly. Subsection 3 of section 23 states:

> Nothing in this Act shall be construed as preventing a patient who requires treatment for mental disorder from being admitted to any hospital or nursing home for that treatment in pursuance of arrangements made in that behalf without any application, recommendation or order rendering him liable to be detained under this Act, or from remaining in any hospital in pursuance of such arrangements if he has ceased to be so liable to be detained.

This is similar to section 5 of the England and Wales Act.

Emergency admission   In Scotland, under section 31 of the Act, a patient can be admitted compulsorily to hospital in an emergency in very much the same way as in England and Wales, except that the period of detention must not exceed seven days. All that is required is the recommendation of a medical practitioner who examined the patient on the day when the recommendation was made. The patient then has to be admitted to hospital within a period of three days from the date of the application.

Where practicable the consent of a relative or of a mental health officer should be obtained, and the recommendation should be accompanied by a statement to that effect. If consent has not been obtained an explanation must be provided. Subsection 5 states that where practicable it is the duty of the board of management to inform the nearest relative without delay that the patient has been admitted to hospital.

Detention of patients already in hospital   Section 32 gives the same powers as section 30 of the England and Wales Act, and makes it possible for a patient already in hospital to be detained compulsorily for a period, here for seven days. The process is similar to admission under section 31, except, of course, that the patient is already in hospital.

Admission and detention of patients Section 24 of the Act is the equivalent of section 26 of the England and Wales Act. There is no equivalent of section 25. An application for admission can be made either by the nearest relative of the patient or by a mental health officer. The application, supported by two medical recommendations, should be addressed to the board of managers of the hospital to which admission is sought. Medical recommendations must be made on the prescribed form and each must include:

(a) a statement of the form of mental disorder from which the patient is suffering, being mental illness or mental deficiency or both;

(b) a statement that the said disorder requires or is susceptible to medical treatment and is of a nature or degree which warrants the patient's detention in a hospital for such treatment; and

(c) a statement that the interests of the health or safety of the patient or the protection of other persons cannot be secured otherwise than by such detention as aforesaid.

As in the case of England and Wales, one of the medical recommendations must be prepared by a doctor recognized by the regional hospital board as having special experience in the diagnosis or treatment of mental disorder. The other doctor should preferably be the patient's general practitioner.

The application and recommendations must be submitted for the sheriff's approval within seven days of the last examination of the patient. In considering the application, the sheriff may make such enquiries and hear from such persons, including the patient, as he thinks fit; where an application is subject to objection by the nearest relative, he must afford that relative, and any witnesses he or she may call, an opportunity of being heard.

When an application for admission has been approved by the sheriff, the patient must be taken into hospital within seven days. It is then the duty of the hospital's board of managers or of the local health authority concerned to notify the Mental Welfare Commission of the admission and to provide them with a copy of the application and medical recommendations. The responsible medical officer must examine the patient or obtain a report from another medical practitioner within seven days. If the patient is to be detained for more than twenty-eight days the Mental Welfare Commission, the patient's nearest relative and the board of managers or local health authority have to be informed. Where the responsible medical officer does recommend continued detention, the order remains in force for up to a year from the day when the patient was first admitted.

If further detention is thought necessary, the responsible medical officer must, in the two months before the current detention order expires, obtain a report to this effect from another medical officer. Here the Scottish legislation differs significantly from that in force in England and Wales, where all that is needed is a report from the responsible medical officer. The patient can then be detained for another year, following which the order may be renewed at two-yearly intervals. Each renewal under Scottish legislation must be supported by a report from a medical practitioner other than the responsible medical officer.

Guardianship
The Mental Health (Scotland) Act makes similar provision for guardianship as does the England and Wales Act, except that the guardianship order has to be made in a way similar to a compulsory admission to hospital order under section 24. Interestingly, section 29 subsection 6 of the Act states specifically that guardians of patients must not administer corporal punishment to them; if they do they are liable on summary conviction to fines of up to fifty pounds. No such protection is provided by the England and Wales Act.

Mentally disordered persons found in public places
Section 104 of the Act follows the phrasing of section 136 of the England and Wales Act, but has an additional subsection. Section 104 allows a constable to remove anyone he considers to be mentally ill from a place to which the public has access to a place of safety. There they may be detained for a period not exceeding seventy-two hours. The additional item in the Mental Health (Scotland) Act is subsection 3, which states: 'where a patient is removed as aforesaid it shall, where practicable, be the duty of the constable who has so removed him, without delay, to inform some responsible person residing

with the patient and the nearest relative of the patient, of that removal'.

Part 5 of the Act, like part 5 of the England and Wales Act, deals with patients involved in criminal proceedings and the transfer of patients under sentence. Section 54 under this part of the Act deals with an individual who is appearing before a court charged with an offence, where under normal circumstances there would be a remand, or a committal for trial. If the court considers that the individual is suffering from a mental disorder that could be dealt with under part 4 of the Act, and a hospital is willing to accept him or her, an order can be made for admission to hospital. This order must be based on written or oral evidence from a medical practitioner.

Powers of courts to order hospital admission or guardianship
Section 55, the equivalent of section 60 in the England and Wales Act, empowers a court to commit a convicted prisoner to a mental hospital. There must be reports by two doctors, one of whom is recognized as having a special knowledge of mental illness. A guardianship order can be made instead of a committal to hospital. Subsection 7 states specifically that a recommendation for committal to a state hospital can be made only if there is medical evidence that the offender is dangerous, violent, or has criminal tendencies that require conditions of special security unavailable in other types of hospital. A state hospital is the equivalent of what is described as a special hospital in the England and Wales Act.

Restriction on discharge
As in England and Wales, a court may place a restriction on the patient's discharge. Section 60 of the Act empowers a court to restrict discharge so that patients can only be discharged or allowed out on leave on the authority of the Secretary of State for Scotland. It is almost identical to section 65 of the Mental Health Act 1959, except that people are allowed to appeal in the same way as they can appeal against a conviction. This applies to a hospital order without restriction and to a guardianship order or hospital order with restriction.

Removal to hospital of prisoners
Section 66 makes it possible for a convicted prisoner to be transferred to hospital if he or she is suffering from a mental disorder which requires such a move. It is the equivalent of section 72 of the Mental Health Act 1959.

Fitness to plead
Section 63 of the Act deals with people who are unfit to plead and makes provision for their admission to hospital with a restriction on discharge without limit of time.

Appeals
There are no Mental Health Review Tribunals in Scotland, but patients compulsorily detained in hospital can appeal to the Sheriff's Court.

From this brief account of mental health legislation in Scotland it can be seen that there are a number of differences between the law in Scotland and in England and Wales. Some of these differences favour the patient and in theory offer him or her more protection. But in practice there is little real difference between procedures for hospital admission in Scotland and in England and Wales.

11 Mental Health Legislation in Northern Ireland

The Mental Health Act (Northern Ireland) 1961 is broadly similar to the Act dealing with mental illness for England and Wales. There are certain differences, however, such as the periods of compulsory detention specified for observation and treatment, and in cases of emergency. Psychopathy is not mentioned in the Northern Ireland Act and so it is not legally possible to detain compulsorily people suffering from it in Northern Ireland. This seems reasonable in so far as most psychiatrists believe that psychopathy is not susceptible to psychiatric treatment, and in fact moves are now in hand to change the England and Wales Act. However, contrary to some people's expectations, the Mental Health (Amendment) Bill does not actually exclude psychopathy.

As one might expect, the various sections are differently numbered in the Acts, something that can cause considerable confusion when one compares the two pieces of legislation. For example, section 25 of the English Act deals with compulsory admission of patients to hospital for observation, while section 25 of the Northern Ireland Act is concerned with patients' correspondence.

The important differences between the two Acts are considered below.

Special care services

In Northern Ireland, services for the mentally handicapped are described as special care services, and the patient is described as a special care case. The Northern Ireland Hospital Authority, referred to in the Act as 'The Authority', is instructed to make provisions for special care cases. Powers are provided for their compulsory admission to hospital and submission to guardianship, the same powers as those that apply to the mentally ill.

Section 10 of the Act contains powers to compel children considered to be special care cases to attend training centres, and establishes penalties for failure to attend, ranging from a fine not exceeding £1 for the first offence, to a fine not exceeding £10, or imprisonment for a term not exceeding one month, for third and subsequent offences. These offences and penalties naturally apply to the parent or guardian, not the child.

Informal admission to hospital
This Act makes the same assumptions as that governing England and Wales regarding informal admission. Section 6 of the Act, which is worth quoting in full as it does differ slightly in wording, covers this issue:

(1) Nothing in this Act shall be construed as preventing a patient who requires treatment for mental disorder from being admitted to any hospital or private hospital, or from making use of any of the services provided under this Act for persons requiring special care, in pursuance of arrangements made in that behalf and without any notice, application, order or direction rendering him liable to be detained or so treated under this Act, or from remaining in any hospital or private hospital or being treated as such a person in pursuance of such arrangements after he has ceased to be liable to be so detained or treated.

(2) Where an infant who has attained the age of sixteen years is capable of expressing his own wishes any such arrangements as are mentioned in subsection (1) may be made, carried out and determined notwithstanding any right of custody or control vested by law in his parent or guardian.

Compulsory admission to hospital
Section 12 of the Act provides powers for the compulsory admission of a patient to hospital and his or her detention for a period not exceeding twenty-one days from the day of admission. The application can be made by either the nearest relative or the welfare officer. In Northern Ireland, social workers with special responsibilities for mental health are technically known as duly authorized officers, but are generally called welfare officers. Applications must be supported by a medical report on a prescribed form. This must include a statement, backed by reasons, that in the opinion of the practitioner certain conditions apply, and

must explain whether other methods of dealing with the
patient are available, and, if so, why they are not appropriate.
The conditions I have just mentioned relate to the grounds
laid down in the Act for using compulsion. These are:

(a) that the patient is suffering from mental illness, or that he
requires special care, and
(b) that the mental disorder from which he is suffering is of a
nature or degree which warrants his detention in hospital,
and
(c) that it is necessary that he should be so detained in the
interests of his own health or safety, or for the protection
of other persons.

The medical recommendation should preferably be given
by the patient's own medical practitioner, or another practitioner who has a previous acquaintance with the patient.
A special knowledge of psychiatry is not necessary. The
practitioner must examine the patient no more than two days
before signing the recommendation.

Emergency application
Section 15 of the Act allows a welfare officer or any relative
of a patient to apply for admission to hospital in an emergency.
The application must be founded on the same recommendations for admission that apply under section 12, but must
contain a statement to the effect that because the situation is
so urgent, to comply with all the provisions would cause too
great a delay. An emergency application lasts for seven days
from the date of admission to hospital, but the patient can be
detained for a further period under the provisions of section
19 of the Act.

Further provisions as to period of detention
Section 19 of the Act is the equivalent of section 26 of the
England and Wales Act in that it makes it possible for a patient
to be detained for a period longer than twenty-one days. If a
patient has been admitted under section 12 or 15, and it is
considered that he or she should remain in hospital for a
longer period, a doctor approved by the authority can submit
a report recommending detention. The patient must be
examined by the doctor not earlier than fourteen days before

and not later than twenty-one days after the date of admission. The doctor's report must state:

(a) that, in his opinion, the patient is suffering from mental disorder of a nature or degree which warrants his detention in hospital; and

(b) that, in his opinion, it is necessary that the patient should be so detained in the interests of his own health or safety, or for the protection of other persons; and

(c) such particulars as may be prescribed of the grounds for this opinion so far as it relates to the conditions set out in paragraph (a); and

(d) the reasons for this opinion so far as it relates to the conditions set out in paragraph (b), specifying whether other methods of dealing with the patient are available, and if so, why they are not appropriate in this case.

Detention of informal patients

Section 16 of the Act empowers the medical practitioner in charge of the treatment of an informal patient to detain that patient for a period not exceeding three days, in the same way that this is done under section 30 of the England and Wales Act.

Mentally disordered persons found in public places

Section 106, almost identical to section 136 of the England and Wales Act, gives power to a constable to remove an individual whom he considers to be mentally ill, and who is found in a place to which the public have access, to a place of safety, and there detain that person for a period not exceeding seventy-two hours.

Guardianship

Guardianship is dealt with in virtually the same way as in the England and Wales Act, requiring a report from two medical practitioners, one of whom must be appointed by the authority. The guardian appointed then has the same powers over the patient as if he were the father and the patient a child of fourteen years.

Admission of patients concerned in criminal proceedings
The Northern Ireland Act deals with criminally ill offenders
in a similar way to the England and Wales Act. Section 48
resembles section 60 of the England and Wales Act, while
section 53 gives powers to the court to place a restriction on
discharge, as does section 65 of the England and Wales legislation. When someone is dealt with under section 48 of the
Act, the same conditions apply that operate under section 12.
The court may order the patient to be detained in hospital or
taken into guardianship.

In the case of a restriction order, the patient can only be
discharged, transferred to another hospital, or given privileges
on an order from the Minister of Home Affairs, referred to in
the Act as 'The Minister'. The patient is not allowed to appeal
to a Mental Health Review Tribunal, but the Minister may
direct a Mental Health Review Tribunal to examine the patient
and report its findings. When a patient is dealt with under
sections 48 and 53, he or she can make an appeal against the
order in the same manner as against a conviction.

Section 56 deals with individuals who are found to be unfit
to stand trial either before the trial commences or during the
course of the trial by a jury empanelled for the purpose. The
court must direct a finding to that effect and order the
person's admission to hospital. Under these circumstances
the patient is treated as if an order under section 48 and 53
had been made to place a restriction on discharge without
limit of time.

Section 58 empowers the Minister to order the transfer to
hospital of a mentally ill prisoner serving a sentence. This
order has the same effect as a hospital order, but if the Minister
considers a restriction on discharge is necessary, he can use
powers under section 60, which are the same as those provided
under section 53.

Mental Health Review Tribunals
The Mental Health Review Tribunals for Northern Ireland are
similar to their equivalents in England and Wales. The third
schedule of the Act deals with the constitution of a Mental
Health Review Tribunal, while sections 76–79 deal with
applications and powers.

Patients' rights

On the whole patients have similar rights (and lack of them) in Northern Ireland and in England and Wales. However, there are some significant differences. Section 25 deals with the correspondence of patients:

> It shall be the duty of a management committee, a person carrying on a private hospital or a person appointed as guardian under this Part to forward unopened all letters addressed by any patient liable to be detained or subject to guardianship under this Part to —
>
> the Lord Chief Justice;
> the Minister of Health and Local Government;
> any member of Parliament;
> the Review Tribunal;
> the Ministry;
> the Registrar of the Department for the Affairs of Mental Patients;
> the nearest relative of the patient.

As we have seen, section 36 of the England and Wales Act gives the responsible medical officer specific powers to intercept postal packets, but also makes it clear that packets addressed to certain individuals, such as the Secretary of State for Health, cannot be intercepted. The Northern Ireland Act does not have the same provision, though section 25 does imply that packages sent to people other than those mentioned may be intercepted.

The most important difference between the two Acts, as far as patients' rights are concerned, relates to protection for the staff of mental hospitals or others involved in implementing the Act, such as social workers. To recap, in the England and Wales Act, section 141 prevents patients from taking civil or criminal proceedings against the staff of psychiatric hospitals, or others who may have been involved in carrying out duties under the Act, without first obtaining the leave of the High Court. The High Court is not allowed to give permission unless satisfied that there are substantial grounds that the person to be proceeded against has acted in bad faith or without reasonable care. Section 111 of the Northern Ireland Act provides that:

> (1) A person shall not be liable, whether on the ground of want of jurisdiction or on any other ground, to any civil or criminal

proceedings to which he would have been liable apart from this section in respect of any act purporting to be done in pursuance of this Act, or any regulations or rules thereunder, unless the act was done in bad faith or without reasonable care.

(2) Civil or criminal proceedings shall not be brought against any person in any court in respect of any such act without the leave of the Supreme Court, and the Supreme Court shall not give leave under this section unless satisfied that there is a prima facie case for the contention that the person to be proceeded against has acted in bad faith or without reasonable care.

(3) This section does not apply to proceedings for an offence under this Act, being proceedings which are instituted by, or by the direction of, the Attorney General or proceedings under section 99, 100, or 101.

Thus in Northern Ireland the Supreme Court can give leave if it is satisfied that there is a prima facie case – that is, one based on an immediate impression – to support the contention that the person to be proceeded against has acted in bad faith or without reasonable care. There is clearly a significant difference between 'substantial grounds' and a 'prima facie case'.

On the whole the Northern Ireland Act and the England and Wales Act are quite similar, but the former does have certain advantages that benefit patients in Northern Ireland.

12 Suggested Changes
   in the Law

The Mental Health Act of 1959 fostered many of the beneficial changes that have occurred in our treatment, understanding and support of the mentally ill. However, after it became law criticisms were made, and during the past decade many people have suggested that changes and modifications are necessary. As well as concern about mental health legislation there has been concern about the treatment of mentally ill offenders. Because of these anxieties a committee was set up under Lord Butler (the Committee on Mentally Abnormal Offenders, also known as the Butler Committee) to examine the problems involved. It produced a report in October 1975, and in 1979 the Department of Health and Social Security issued a White Paper entitled 'Review of the Mental Health Act' in an attempt to deal with some of the problems created by the Act of 1959.

The Report of the Butler Committee and the Review of the Mental Health Act are wholly different documents. The Butler Report exposed many problems and put forward recommendations for substantial change in the law on mentally ill offenders. The Review of the Mental Health Act tended to the view that the Mental Health Act of 1959 was a good piece of legislation that had been successfully implemented, and that required only mild modification.

It is not possible to describe and examine the Report of the Butler Committee in detail here, but it is important reading for anyone interested in mental health legislation. I shall consider some of its recommendations, since it is possible that they may be implemented in the foreseeable future. One that was immediately accepted was for the establishment of Regional Secure Units for mentally ill offenders. Since the report's publication the Department of Health and Social Security has been attempting to establish such units in the various regions of the Health Service: to date, some have been built, but none are fully operational. The purpose of such units was to provide a secure environment in which mentally ill offenders could be treated and rehabilitated without having to be committed to one of the special hospitals. It was also intended that patients could be transferred to such units when they no longer needed the degree of security provided by the special hospitals. Opinion has been divided about Regional Secure Units. Some critics claim that they would simply become minor special hospitals with no advantages of their own, while other people believe that the establishment of such units will facilitate the treatment and rehabilitation of offenders and make their aftercare more effective and reliable.

The Butler Report deals with fitness to plead, the special verdict, hospital orders and restriction orders, and introduces the idea of an interim hospital order. The proposed special verdict 'not guilty on evidence of mental disorder' is an attempt to improve upon the McNaghten Rules, the Durham Formula and the American Law Institute Model Penal Code Test. The Butler Committee also proposed that the court should have greater discretion on disposal, including the power to discharge the defendant. At present a special verdict, like a finding of unfitness to plead or stand trial, entails automatic detention under a restriction order.

With regard to hospital orders, the committee suggested the introduction of a criterion of 'benefit from treatment' for offenders classified as psychopathic or subnormal (mentally handicapped). The question here, of course, is precisely what is meant by 'benefit from treatment'. The White Paper on the review of the Mental Health Act covers this issue and produces a broad definition of treatment: 'care, training, the use of habilitative techniques and medical, nursing and other professional help'. Such a definition is unhelpful, but another Butler Committee recommendation offers a possible solution, the interim hospital order. The idea of an interim hospital order is that a mentally ill offender can be committed to a psychiatric hospital, special hospital or Regional Secure Unit for a period of three months, with a possibility of further month-by-month extensions up to a maximum of six months. This order would permit a fuller assessment of the patient's mental state and potential for treatment, while in the case of someone who is unfit to plead it would allow for treatment that might result in his or her later becoming fit to plead.

The Mental Health (Amendment) Bill follows the recommendations of the Butler Committee exactly in providing for interim hospital orders. These would last for up to twelve weeks initially but could be renewed for further periods of up to twenty-eight days at a time within an overall limit of six months.

The problem of an accused person who is unfit to be tried or unfit to plead is a grave one, since at present he or she might be committed to a psychiatric establishment with a restriction on discharge without limit of time, when in fact he or she may be innocent of the alleged offence. The Butler Committee tackled this problem by recommending that there should be a full trial of the facts, enabling the jury to return a verdict of not guilty when the evidence was not sufficient for a conviction. Under an interim hospital order it would also be possible to commit the accused to hospital for treatment with the objective of improving his or her condition sufficiently for trial; this would also offer the opportunity to assess the patient's likely response to treatment.

If the Mental Health (Amendment) Bill becomes law it will introduce some important changes, but sadly it has neglected a number of problems that have been troubling reformers for some time. I have outlined the most important proposals in discussing the details of the current legislation, and I will summarize them here to give an idea of the scope of the Bill.

Psychopathic disorder has not been removed from the Act, but it has been redefined to exclude any mention of susceptibility to medical treatment. However, there is a complementary change in section 26 which states that a patient may be compulsorily detained in the case of psychopathic disorder (or mental handicap) if treatment is likely to alleviate or prevent a deterioration of the patient's condition.

Section 25 of the new Bill is now concerned with 'Admission for Assessment', the word 'assessment' having been substituted for 'observation'. It proposes that patients detained under this section should be allowed to apply to a Mental Health Review Tribunal, and thus would make it possible for all compulsorily detained patients to apply to a Tribunal, except for those detained under section 29.

Some changes are proposed in the definition of the nearest relative. Mothers and fathers are made equal in the hierarchy, and applications for compulsory detention under the new Bill would be made by the relative(s) with whom the patient was living.

I have discussed changes in the law regarding mentally disordered offenders in chapter 6. Restriction orders, currently carried out for 'the protection of the public', would have to satisfy the condition of protecting the public from 'serious harm'.

MentalHealth Review Tribunals would largely operate under the same conditions as at present. However, if detained patients did not themselves apply to the Tribunal within the application period, the managers of their hospitals would have to refer their cases for review. The Bill also spells out the patient's right to have an independent medical opinion, something that has generally been allowed in practice even though it is not specified in the principal Act.

The Amendment Bill provides for the establishment of a Mental Health Act Commission made up of lawyers, doctors, nurses, psychologists, social workers and members of the public. Its function would be similar to that of the Scottish Mental Welfare Commission (see chapter 10), and its particular concerns would be detained patients and the difficult issue of treatment against patients' wishes.

Consent to treatment has always been a problem, and it was hoped that new legislation would establish panels including doctors, lawyers, nurses, social workers and laymen to adjudicate in cases where a doctor decides treatment should be given against a patient's wishes. This would be especially important if the treatment was irreversible (e.g. leucotomy), hazardous, or of dubious efficacy. Emergency treatments might have to be given without consulting the panel, but it would have to be informed of them. The Amendment Bill does not actually go this far: the Mental Health Act Commission would appoint a doctor rather than a panel to provide a second opinion on treatment against patients' wishes. Other functions of the Commission would be to draw up a list of treatments that give rise to special concern, and to elaborate a code of conduct.

Hospital patients' freedom to communicate would be improved under the new Bill; interference with informal patients' mail would be prohibited altogether and interception of detained patients' mail would be restricted further than the current Act permits.

The Mental Health Act of 1959 replaced mental welfare officers with approved social workers; the Bill makes it clear that these social workers ought to be approved by the social service authority, which must be satisfied that they are competent in dealing with people suffering from mental disorders.

The Mental Health (Amendment) Bill is certainly a step in the right direction, but it does contain some serious omissions. It fails, for example, to tackle the reform of section 141 of the principal Act, and does not deal with the rights of a restricted patient to have his or her case scrutinized by an independent court. However, perhaps appropriate amendments will be made during debate to make this a genuinely effective act of reform. (See Postscript, p. 137.)

13 Mental Health and the Law

In the previous chapter some possible changes in mental health legislation were discussed. While these suggestions have yet to be implemented, some people hold that many further changes are necessary. The very concept of mental illness is open to question. Some people take the view that mental illness, in the medical sense, does not exist. Others consider that almost all abnormal behaviour is explicable in medical terms and has physical causes. Between these two extremes there are many shades of grey; among those who dismiss the medical model there are a variety of non-medical explanations on offer. In fact, what we call 'mental illness' covers a great spectrum of problems, types of behaviour, emotional reactions, mental processes and ways of life. Theories abound, but facts are hard to come by, and it is possible to develop speculations and explanations quite unencumbered by the discipline of science.

In this book, the orthodox view of mental illness has been broadly accepted because this view is the one usually advanced when considering the application of law to mental illness. The orthodox view accepts the existence of both organically induced mental illness and that caused by emotional and social factors. All the same, we should bear in mind that the orthodox view may be quite wrong — and so may any other of our current explanations. This is not a plea for anarchy, simply for keeping an open mind, though that can have its disadvantages too, particularly when decisions have to be made. But this is a problem that everyone who is involved in mental health matters has to confront and tackle.

If mental illness is in fact a medical problem, it is regrettable that there is any legal involvement in the subject beyond the normal impact of the law on human behaviour. Specific mental health legislation differentiates mental illness from physical illness merely by its existence. Of course, legislation relating to physical illness also exists, but it deals with specific, limited issues and does not attempt to be as inclusive, as does the law with regard to mental disorder. The existence of mental health legislation thus becomes a problem in itself, and, perhaps as a result, generates many other difficulties.

Some people believe that there should be no specific mental health legislation: the mentally ill, or rather those we now call 'mentally ill', should be either left alone by the processes of law or dealt with under existing, non-mental health legislation. Under this scheme it would not be possible to admit a patient compulsorily to hospital, but it would be possible to arrest a mentally ill person who committed an offence and then deal with him or her in the usual way, just as if he or she were not mentally ill. There are several good reasons for supporting this view, including the prospect that the normal legal process might be much less likely to cause an abuse of personal liberty than mental health legislation is. As I have suggested, this belief is not without foundation, since mental health legislation does make it possible to deprive individuals of their liberty quite easily, and subsequently to deprive them of many of the protections and possibilities of redress that would be applicable if action were taken under criminal or civil law.

To most people it seems absurd to deny the reality of mental illness, even more so when the denial is supported by arguments about the law and personal liberty. On the whole it seems more reasonable to accept that individuals can become 'mentally ill', and to accept that this condition, whatever its origins, may lead to odd, irrational, sometimes dangerous behaviour which makes specific legislation necessary to protect both the sufferers and the general public. If this legislation then appears to offend against ideals of individual liberty and justice it needs to be changed, not abolished.

In previous chapters I have examined examples of defects in the law and shown how the Mental Health Acts of England and Wales, Scotland and Northern Ireland differ from each other, with each possessing certain advantages over the others. A degree of amalgamation, or perhaps a little imitation, might thus help to produce a general improvement.

As well as the changes recommended by the Butler Committee and the Mental Health (Amendment) Bill, the following modifications are worth considering. Perhaps they might prompt further discussions among all those involved in mental illness and the law, and one would hope that reforms might be suggested and implemented that, while accepting the need to protect society, would further guarantee the individual's liberty.

Regardless of his or her knowledge of mental illness, a doctor can have anyone admitted to a mental hospital and detained there for up to three days. There is no appeal against this action, and neither the individual nor his or her family and friends can do anything about it. In theory an application can be made for a writ of habeas corpus, but this is not really a practicable proposition. It is possible to argue that the staff of a psychiatric institution can refuse to admit someone they consider to be wrongly handled under the Act, or they can discharge him or her on admittance. In reality, though, the only person involved with admissions may be an inexperienced junior doctor, who is likely to accept patients and keep them in hospital until they have been seen by a more senior doctor, which may not be until the end of the three day period.

All this is painting perhaps too gloomy a picture; in reality, malicious abuse of these powers and provisions rarely occurs. The risk is there, however, and many patients are unnecessarily admitted to hospital under compulsion. Compulsion is some-times used before other methods have even been tried; there are still psychiatric hospitals in the United Kingdom that do not accept informal admissions in the evenings or at weekends, and there are many family doctors who believe that the use of compulsion eases the process of admission. It can be remarkably difficult to get someone admitted into a mental hospital even when there are strong grounds and the patient expresses a desire to enter and receive treatment. Possible reasons include a shortage of facilities in some areas of the country, and a certain amount of bloodymindedness on the part of some staff. Under these conditions it is understandable for a family doctor to attempt to use compulsion. But even the presentation of compulsory forms does not compel a hospital to take a patient, something that ought to be made known to all family doctors.

A constable, as we have seen, can compulsorily remove

someone from a public place and detain him or her for up to
three days in a place of safety. The use of this legislation
varies from area to area: in some places these powers are rarely
if ever put into practice, while in others they are used quite
frequently.

It does seem that the individual needs more protection
than currently exists where compulsory admission to hospital
is concerned. To take the police powers first, it would seem
sensible to reduce the period of detention to, perhaps, six
hours, as distinct from seventy-two hours. Then anyone
considered to be mentally ill who had been apprehended by a
constable in a public place would have to be seen within six
hours by an experienced psychiatrist. Certainly, if you were
involved in an accident you would expect to be seen within
six hours by a doctor or surgeon; a long delay would be totally
unacceptable. Yet a psychiatric crisis can cause someone to
lose his or her liberty for three days without any obligation
on the authorities to provide expert psychiatric attention.
The provision of an adequate psychiatric service is surely the
main priority when we consider changing the present
legislation, as I shall argue later.

Since people sometimes do become deeply disturbed and
in consequence can become a danger to themselves or others,
it is essential to have legislation which allows them to be
helped compulsorily. Sometimes help has to be provided
quickly, so there is no sense in having cumbersome mechanisms
to prevent the inappropriate use of compulsion if these
measures expose mentally ill people and the general public to
unnecessary dangers. One solution would be to establish a
system of accountability, so that every doctor who used
compulsion – be it under section 29 of the England and
Wales Act or its equivalents in other parts of the United
Kingdom – would have to explain his or her actions to a
group made up of a doctor, a social worker, a lawyer and a
member of the public. The procedure would be informal, but
there should be provision for a more formal enquiry if abuse
had occurred. While such a reform would be unpopular with
doctors, it is a question of individual liberty that is at stake,
and I believe that, once established, such a system would be
quickly accepted. If doctors knew they would have to explain

their actions later, the few who do at present misuse their legal powers would think again. Failing that, the warning that would be delivered by the examining group, coupled with the threat of a formal enquiry if subsequent offences occurred, would prevent further abuse.

The Mental Health (Amendment) Bill provides for the establishment of a Mental Health Act Committee similar in composition to the group I have proposed, but a central commission would clearly not be able to deal with doctors' use of compulsion in the way I have suggested. Regional commissions would perhaps be created to take on this role if the law was changed appropriately.

The establishment of informal status was an important change in mental health legislation, but it has been accompanied by certain dangers. When someone is admitted to a psychiatric establishment as an informal patient, there are no legally established mechanisms for reviewing his or her case, or for investigating the need for continued residence. Thus patients may enter hospital informally and stay there for the rest of their lives unless the doctor responsible for their care discharges them or they ask to be discharged. It is easy to become institutionalized, though some people are more susceptible than others; for this and other reasons — apathy, fear of authority, and so on — people may remain in hospital even when they no longer desire or need to remain. It would be helpful to review informal patients regularly and establish procedures to ensure that the responsible medical officer is asked to explain why someone has stayed in hospital for a long time. Many mental hospitals are still large places where it is surprisingly easy to be forgotten. Simply because someone has been neglected and does not make a fuss does not mean that he or she still needs to stay in an institution. I have discharged many people in this position who were delighted to discover that life was still possible outside their institution in a world the rest of us often take for granted.

The rights of patients in hospital are just as important as the protection of freedom outside institutions. It is not only a question of the length of detention but also of what happens during it. The right to take criminal or civil action against people who have harmed you has been discussed in chapter 8.

The Northern Ireland Act seems to be superior to the others in this respect, but all place restrictions on patients that do not apply to other citizens. Granted, it is distressing to staff to have frivolous litigation brought against them, but so it is for any citizen, and it is hard to understand why the staff of psychiatric hospitals – like the staff of prisons – should be specially protected. In fact, the European Court has ruled that the protection of prison staff should cease, though no action has yet been taken. There are thus strong arguments in favour of repealing the legislation that prevents patients from taking action against staff without official authorization. This matter has been ignored in the Mental Health (Amendment) Bill, except for a mention in the accompanying White Paper.

It also seems quite wrong to allow medical officers to interfere with patients' correspondence and to deprive them of voting rights simply because they are resident in psychiatric hospitals. As we have seen, the new Bill does tackle the question of patients' correspondence, though perhaps the reforms are not as thorough as some people had hoped. The whole question of patients' rights needs careful examination; reforms must be devised to ensure that the facts of mental illness and institutional care do not create second class citizens who lack rights that are automatic for the rest of us.

Mental Health Review Tribunals exist to protect patients against the inappropriate use of compulsory detention. Here the most urgent reform is to make it obligatory for patients appearing before a tribunal to be provided with expert help. This would not only benefit the patient but also make the work of the tribunal easier, more effective and more just.

The role of the Court of Protection is an important one, and it does seem that many people would benefit, particularly the more seriously disabled, if the court could take over their affairs, so that the money they have could be spent to their advantage without fears of misuse or misappropriation. To allow this, the Court of Protection's staff would have to be enlarged, and arrangements would need to be made for receivers to be appointed. The latter problem could be handled by local authority social services departments, provided staff were made available. This problem chiefly affects long-stay patients in institutions, who are unable to benefit from their small incomes because they are unable to spend the money themselves, and institutional staff are forbidden to spend it for them.

The problem of the mentally ill offender, and the presence of mentally ill individuals in prison, are complex and important matters. The more conspicuous problems at present concern the numbers of mentally ill people in prison, the difficulty of obtaining places in special hospitals for the mentally ill, and the problems of rehabilitating individuals who are in special hospitals. It has been claimed that there are about 500 people in prison who should really be in psychiatric establishments; there may be just as many patients inappropriately detained in special hospitals.

The use of section 65, and its equivalents in the Scotland and Northern Ireland Acts, is a cause for some anxiety. Section 65 places severe restrictions on both doctor and patient, since the doctor cannot grant leave or discharge the patient without obtaining permission from the Home Office. This is one of the reasons why individuals dealt with under section 60/65 are not admitted to district psychiatric hospitals. It can rightly be argued that the use of section 65 is a method of protecting the public against dangerous people suffering from severe mental disturbance, and no one would deny the need for such protection. However, there is a tendency to use section 65 to deal with mentally ill offenders of all kinds, many of whom are not at all dangerous, although they may be a nuisance. If the use of section 65 was rigorously limited to cases where people are genuinely dangerous, some of the problems presented by mentally ill offenders would be solved. I have treated people handled under section 60/65 who were relatively harmless and had committed quite minor offences, such as obtaining meals by deceit and stealing a purse from a house. I believe that such cases constitute gross misuse of this section of the Mental Health Act by the courts.

Another current problem in the treatment of mentally ill offenders is the resistance of district psychiatric hospitals to accepting this kind of patient. The overuse of section 65 is one cause; another is the resistance of nursing staff, who object to dealing with mentally ill offenders, firstly because some of them may be violent, and secondly because their colleagues in special hospitals receive substantially higher wages for looking after such patients. As a result of this resistance patients are not accepted from court or on transfer from special hospitals, leaving special hospitals overfull and with little chance of transferring individuals for further rehabilitation. So the courts are often forced to send people to prison who really ought to be sent to hospital.

If we try to look objectively at mental illness, mental health services and the law, one thing is plain. If there are well-developed psychiatric services geared to help people within the community, providing a service twenty-four hours a day, seven days a week, there is little need to use the compulsory powers provided by mental health legislation. When the service is poor, compulsion will be used more extensively on mentally ill offenders and non-offenders alike. Before considering reforms in the law, we should first think of improving the services available. This done, reforms are less likely to be necessary. It is a pity that the Mental Health Act does not contain a clear statement of society's obligation to provide proper psychiatric facilities. Given the prevailing principles of legislation and administration, this might prove difficult, but this is no reason to abandon the ideal of legislation that would operate to citizens' benefit, instead of disposing of problems by the use of prohibitions and institutions to isolate people where society can conveniently forget about them.

Local authorities should be compelled to provide adequate community services; the Health Service should be similarly obliged to make its own contribution to the care, support and treatment of the mentally ill. After all, legislation does exist to compel local authorities to take certain action to care for children, as is only right, so it is not as if there are no parallels elsewhere.

At present there are too many powers that can be used against the individual, and too few provisions that ensure accountability of authorities at national and local levels.

Postscript: Progress in the Reform of Mental Health Legislation

The Mental Health (Amendment) Bill was introduced in the House of Lords at the end of 1981 and has already received two readings and been debated in Committee. A number of significant amendments have been put forward which go some way in tackling some of the criticisms of both the main Act and the Amendment Bill.

Mental handicap

Many individuals and organizations have been concerned about mental handicap being equated with mental illness. As it stood, the Amendment Bill did not deal adequately with this problem, but a Government amendment will make it clear that mentally handicapped people are not to be bound by the provisions of the Mental Health Act unless they also have associated 'abnormally aggressive or seriously irresponsible conduct'. Thus mental handicap, in itself, will at least not be legally viewed as an illness.

Section 141

The Amendment Bill did not deal with section 141 of the main Act, despite the fact that a case concerning this section was recently referred to the European Commission of Human Rights. Section 141 severely restricts mental patients' rights to sue hospital staff. An amendment to the Bill repealing section 141 has now been tabled.

Section 65

The Amendment Bill did not suggest any reform of section 65, thus leaving the power to discharge a patient solely in the hands of the Home Secretary.

The Government has tabled an amendment that would allow patients detained under section 65 to appeal to a Mental Health Review Tribunal, which would have the power to discharge them. However, under the second part of this amendment patients detained under section 60/65 would not be allowed to apply to a tribunal until they had been detained for six months, and the same ruling would apply to patients detained under section 60. At present patients detained under section 60 *can* apply to a Mental Health Review Tribunal in the first six months of their detention. While it is understandable that there should be a restriction on patients detained under section 60/65, it is difficult to know why the rights of patients detained under section 60 alone should also have to suffer.

It seems likely that these amendments will be passed, and that they will be the only significant changes in the form of the Bill.

It is expected that the Amendment Bill will finally take effect from September 1983.

February 1982

Appendix

Some of the Forms Currently in Use

Form I
(Hospital Code 90-541)

MENTAL HEALTH ACT 1959

Application for Admission for Observation (Section 25)

(1) Name and address of hospital or mental nursing home

TO THE MANAGERS OF (¹)...

(2) Name and address of applicant

1. I (²).. of ....
....hereby apply for the admission of

(3) Name and address of patient

(³).. of ....
....to the
above named hospital for observation in accordance with Part IV of the Mental Health Act 1959.

(4) State relationship (see section 49 50 and 51 overleaf)

2.

Delete the TWO statements which do not apply.

(a) I am the patient's nearest relative within the meaning of the Act. being the patient's (⁴)

OR

(5) Copy of the court order or form of authority signed by the nearest relative under Regulation 25 of the Mental Health (Hospital and Guardianship) Regulations 1960

(b) I have been authorised by $\frac{\text{a county court}}{\text{the patient's nearest relative}}$ to exercise the functions of the patient's nearest relative under the Act and a copy (⁵) of the authority is attached to this application.

OR

(6) Name of local social services authority

(c) I am an officer of (⁶)...
appointed to act as mental welfare officer for the purposes of the Act.

3. I last saw the patient on .... 19 ....

4. This application is founded on the medical recommendations forwarded herewith.

(7) If neither of the medical practitioners who have made the medical recommendations had previous acquaintance with the patient, the applicant should state here why it is not practicable to obtain a recommendation from a practitioner having such acquaintance

5. (⁷) ....
....
....
....
....

Signed ....

Date ....

RECORD OF ADMISSION (*This is not part of the application, but is to be completed later at the hospital or mental home.*)

(8) Name of patient

(a) (⁸) ....was admitted to

(9) Name of hospital or mental nursing home

(⁹) ....in pursuance of
this application on... 19 ....

Delete (a) or (b)

OR

(b) (⁸) ....was already an in-patient

in (⁹) ....

on the date of this application and the application was received by me on behalf of the managers

on .... 19 ....

Signed ....
on behalf of the managers

Date ....

MENTAL HEALTH ACT 1959

Definition of Relative and Nearest Relative

Definition of relative and nearest relative

Section 49.—(1) In this Part of this Act "relative", means any of the following, that is to say—

(a) husband or wife;
(b) son or daughter;
(c) father;
(d) mother;
(e) brother or sister;
(f) grandparent;
(g) grandchild;
(h) uncle or aunt;
(i) nephew or niece.

(2) In deducing relationships for the purpose of this section, an adopted person shall be treated as the child of the person or persons by whom he was adopted and not as the child of any other person; and subject as aforesaid, any relationships of the half-blood shall be treated as a relationship of the whole blood, and an illegitimate person shall be treated as the legitimate child of his mother.

(3) In this Part of this Act, subject to the provisions of this section and to the following provisions of this Part of this Act, the "nearest relative" means the person first described in subsection (1) of this section who is for the time being surviving, relatives of the whole blood being preferred to relatives of the same description of the half-blood, and the elder or eldest of two or more relatives described in any paragraph of that subsection being preferred to the other or others of those relatives regardless of sex.

(4) Where the person who, under subsection (3) of this section would be the nearest relative of a patient—

(a) is not ordinarily resident within the United Kingdom; or
(b) being the husband or wife of the patient, is permanently separated from the patient, either by agreement or under an order of a court, or has deserted or has been deserted by the patient for a period which has not come to an end or;
(c) not being the husband, wife, father or mother of the patient, is for the time being under eighteen years of age; or
(d) is a man against whom an order divesting him of authority over the patient has been made under section thirty-eight of the Sexual Offences Act 1956 (which relates to incest with a girl under eighteen) and has not been rescinded,

the nearest relative of the patient shall be ascertained as if that person were dead.

(5) In this section "adoption order" means an order for the adoption of any person made under Part I of the Adoption Act 1958, or any previous enactment relating to the adoption of children, or any corresponding enactment of the Parliament of Northern Ireland, and "court" includes a court in Scotland or Northern Ireland.

(6) In this section "husband" and "wife" include a person who is living with the patient as the patient's husband or wife, as the case may be (or, if the patient is for the time being an in-patient in a hospital, was so living until the patient was admitted), and has been or had been so living for a period of not less than six months; but a person shall not be treated by virtue of this subsection as the nearest relative of a married patient unless the husband or wife of the patient is disregarded by virtue of paragraph (b) of subsection (4) of this section.

Children and young persons in care of local authority.

Section 50. In any case where the rights and powers of a parent of a patient, being a child or a young person, are vested in a local authority or other person by virtue of—

(a) section twenty-four of the Children and Young Persons Act 1969 (which relates to the powers and duties of local authorities with respect to persons committed to their care in pursuance of that Act);
(b) section three of the Children Act 1948 (which relates to children in respect of whom parental rights have been assumed under section 2 of that Act),
(c) section seventeen of the Social Work (Scotland) Act 1968 (which makes corresponding provision for Scotland),

that authority or person shall be deemed to be the nearest relative of the patient in preference to any person except the patient's husband or wife (if any) and except, in a case where the said rights and powers are vested in a local authority by virtue of subsection (2) of the said section three, or subsection (2) of the said section seventeen any parent of the patient not being a person on whose account the resolution mentioned in that subsection was passed.

Nearest relative of infant under guardianship, etc.

Section 51.—(1) Where a patient who has not attained the age of eighteen years—

(a) is, by virtue of an order made by a court in the exercise of jurisdiction (whether under any enactment or otherwise) in respect of the guardianship of infants (including an order under section thirty-eight of the Sexual Offences Act 1956), or by virtue of a deed or will executed by his father or mother, under the guardianship of a person not being his nearest relative under the foregoing provisions of this Act, or is under the joint guardianship of two persons of whom one is such a person as aforesaid; or

(b) is, by virtue of an order made by a court in the exercise of such jurisdiction as aforesaid or in matrimonial proceedings, or by virtue of a separation agreement between his father and mother, in the custody of any such person,

the person or persons having the guardianship or custody of the patient shall, to the exclusion of any other person, be deemed to be his nearest relative.

(2) Subsection (4) of section forty-nine of this Act shall apply in relation to a person who is, or who is one of the persons, deemed to be the nearest relative of a patient by virtue of this section as it applies in relation to a person who would be the nearest relative under subsection (3) of this section.

(3) A patient shall be treated for the purposes of this section as being in the custody of another person if he would be in that other person's custody apart from section thirty-four of this Act.

(4) In this section "court" includes a court in Scotland or Northern Ireland, and "enactment" includes an enactment of the Parliament of Northern Ireland.

Form 3B
(Hospital Code 90-544)

MENTAL HEALTH ACT 1959

Joint Medical Recommendation for Admission for Observation (Section 25)

(1) Names and addresses of both medical practitioners

1. We(¹)... of ....

.... and ....

of ....

(2) Name and address of patient

being registered medical practitioners recommend that (²)..................

of ....

be admitted to a hospital for observation in accordance with Part IV of the Mental Health Act 1959.

(3) Name of first practitioner

2. (a) I(³)... last examined this patient

on...19............ .

*Delete if not applicable

*(b) I was acquainted with the patient previously to conducting that examination.

(4) Name of area health authority

*(c) I have been approved by (⁴)............................... Area Health Authority under Section 28 of the Act as having special experience in the diagnosis or treatment of mental disorder.

(5) Name of second practitioner

3. (a) I(⁵)... last examined this patient

on...19............ .

*Delete if not applicable

*(b) I was acquainted with the patient previously to conducting that examination.

*(c) I have been approved by (⁴)............................... Area Health Authority under Section 28 of the Act as having special experience in the diagnosis or treatment of mental disorder.

(6) Names of both practitioners

4. We(⁶)................................... and...........................

are of the opinion:—

(a) that this patient is suffering from mental disorder of a nature or degree which warrants $\frac{his}{her}$

detention in a hospital under observation for at least a limited period;

AND

(b) that this patient ought to be so detained :—

Delete (i) or (ii) unless both apply

(i) in the interests of the patient's own health or safety;

(ii) with a view to the protection of other persons;

AND

(c) that informal admission is not appropriate in the circumstances of this case.

Signed ....

Date ....

Signed ....

Date ....

Form 3A
(Hospital Code 90-543)

MENTAL HEALTH ACT 1959

Medical Recommendation for Admission for Observation (Section 25 or 29)

(1) Name and address of medical practitioner

1. I (¹).. of ....

being a registered medical

(2) Name and address of patient

practitioner, recommend that (²)..

of..

be admitted to a hospital for observation in accordance with Part IV of the Mental Health Act 1959.

2. I last examined this patient on..19........ .

*Delete if not applicable

3. *(a) I was acquainted with the patient previously to conducting that examination.

(3) Name of Area Health Authority

*(b) I have been approved by (³)..under Section 28

of the Act as having special experience in the diagnosis or treatment of mental disorder.

4. I am of the opinion

(a) that this patient is suffering from mental disorder of a nature or degree which warrants

his
—— detention in a hospital under observation for at least a limited period,
her

AND

(b) that this patient ought to be so detained:

Delete (i) or (ii) unless both apply

(i) in the interests of the patient's own health or safety,
(ii) with a view to the protection of other persons,

AND

(c) that informal admission is not appropriate in the circumstances of this case.

5. (*This section is to be deleted unless the medical recommendation is the first recommendation in support of an emergency application under Section 29.*)

In my opinion it is of urgent necessity for the patient to be admitted and detained under Section 25 of the Act and compliance with the requirements of the Act relating to applications for admission for observation other than emergency applications would involve undesirable delay.

Signed..

Date ....

RECORD OF RECEIPT
(*This is not part of the recommendation, and is to be completed only if the medical recommendation is the second recommendation in support of an emergency application under Section 29.*)

This recommendation was received on behalf of the managers at (⁴)..

(4) Insert time and date

on..19........ the patient having been admitted at (⁴)..

on..19........

Signed ....
on behalf of the managers

Date ....

Form 5B

MENTAL HEALTH ACT 1959

Joint Medical Recommendation for Admission for Treatment (Section 26)

(1) Names and addresses of both medical practitioners

1. We (¹) .... of ....

.... and ....

of ...., being registered

(2) Name and address of patient

medical practitioners, recommend that (²) ....

of.. be admitted to a
hospital for treatment in accordance with Part IV of the Mental Health Act 1959.

(3) Name of first practitioner

2. I (³) .... last examined this patient on

.... 19............

*Delete if not applicable

*I was acquainted with the patient previously to conducting that examination.

(4) Name of area health authority

*I have been approved by (⁴) .... under
Section 28 of the Act as having special experience in the diagnosis or treatment of mental disorder.

(5) Name of second practitioner

3. I (⁵) .... last examined this patient on

.... 19............

*Delete if not applicable

*I was acquainted with the patient previously to conducting that examination.

*I have been approved by (⁴).. under
Section 28 of the Act as having special experience in the diagnosis or treatment of mental disorder.

(6) Names of both practitioners

(7) Insert mental illness, severe subnormality, subnormality and/or psychopathic disorder (see definitions overleaf)

(8) Clinical description of the patient's mental condition

4. We (⁶) .... and .... are of the

opinion that this patient is suffering from (⁷) ....

.... of a nature or degree which warrants $\frac{his}{her}$ detention in a
hospital for medical treatment within the meaning of the Act.   This opinion is founded on the
following grounds:— (⁸)

Delete (i) or (ii) unless both apply

5. *We are of the opinion that it is necessary—
(i) in the interests of this patient's health or safety
(ii) for the protection of other persons

(9) Reasons should indicate whether other methods of care or treatment (e.g. outpatient treatment or local authority services) are available and if so why they are not appropriate, and why informal admission is not suitable

that $\frac{he}{she}$ should be detained in hospital, and our reasons for this opinion are:— (⁹)

Signed ....

Date ....

Signed ....

Date ....

MENTAL HEALTH ACT 195~~9~~

Definition and classification of mental disorder

4.—(1) In this Act "mental disorder" means mental illness, arrested or incomplete development of mind, psychopathic disorder, and any other disorder or disability of mind; and "mentally disordered" shall be construed accordingly.

(2) In this Act "severe subnormality" means a state of arrested or incomplete development of mind which includes subnormality of intelligence and is of such a nature or degree that the patient is incapable of living an independent life or of guarding himself against serious exploitation, or will be so incapable when of an age to do so.

(3) In this Act "subnormality" means a state of arrested or incomplete development of mind (not amounting to severe subnormality) which includes subnormality of intelligence and is of a nature or degree which requires or is susceptible to medical treatment or other special care or training of the patient.

(4) In this Act "psychopathic disorder" means a persistent disorder or disability of mind (whether or not including subnormality of intelligence) which results in abnormally aggressive or seriously irresponsible conduct on the part of the patient, and requires or is susceptible to medical treatment.

(5) Nothing in this section shall be construed as implying that a person may be dealt with under this Act as suffering from mental disorder, or from any form of mental disorder described in this section, by reason only of promiscuity or other immoral conduct.

Form 4A
Hospital Code 90-545

MENTAL HEALTH ACT 1959

Application by Nearest Relative for Admission for Treatment (Section 26)

(1) Name and address of hospital or mental nursing home	TO THE MANAGERS OF(¹) ....
(2) Name and address of applicant	**1.** I(²) .... of .... hereby apply for the admission of
(3) Name and address of patient	(³) .... of .... to the above named hospital for treatment in accordance with Part IV of the Mental Health Act 1959, as a patient suffering from
(4) Insert mental illness, severe sub-normality, and/or psychopathic disorder	(⁴) ....
(5) State relationship (See sections 49, 50 and 51 overleaf)	**2. (a)** I am the patient's nearest relative within the meaning of the Act, being the patient's (⁵) .... **OR**
Delete (a) or (b)	**(b)** I have been authorised by $\dfrac{\text{a county court}}{\text{the patient's nearest relative}}$ to exercise the functions of the patient's
(6) Copy of the court order or of the form of authority signed by the nearest relative under Regulation 25 of the Mental Health (Hospital and Guardianship) Regulations 1960	nearest relative under the Act and a copy of (⁶) the authority is attached to this application. **3.** I last saw the patient on ....19....... **4.** (*This section is to be deleted if the patient is recorded above as suffering from mental illness or severe subnormality.*) **(a)** The patient's date of birth is ....19.......
Delete (a) or (b)	**OR** (if the exact age is not known) **(b)** I believe the patient to be under twenty-one years. **5.** This application is founded on the medical recommendations forwarded herewith.
(7) If neither of the medical practitioners who have made the recommendations had previous acquaintance with the patient, the applicant should state here why it is not practicable to obtain a recommendation from a medical practitioner having such acquaintance	**6.** (⁷) .... Signed .... Date ....

Record of Admission

(*This is not part of the application, but it is to be completed later at the hospital or mental nursing home*).

(8) Name of patient	**(a)** (⁸) .... was admitted to
(9) Name of hospital or mental nursing home	(⁹) .... in pursuance of this application on ....19.......
Delete (a) or (b)	**OR** **(b)** (⁹) .... was already in (⁹) .... on the date of this application and the application was received by me on behalf of the managers on ....19.......

Signed ....
on behalf of the managers

Date ....

MENTAL HEALTH ACT 1959

Definition of Relative and Nearest Relative

Definition of relative and nearest relative

Section 49.—(1) In this Part of this Act "relative", means any of the following, that is to say—

(a) husband or wife;
(b) son or daughter;
(c) father;
(d) mother;
(e) brother or sister;

(f) grandparent;
(g) grandchild;
(h) uncle or aunt;
(i) nephew or niece.

(2) In deducing relationships for the purpose of this section, an adopted person shall be treated as the child of the person or persons by whom he was adopted and not as the child of any other person; and subject as aforesaid, any relationship of the half-blood shall be treated as a relationship of the whole blood, and an illegitimate person shall be treated as the legitimate child of his mother.

(3) In this Part of this Act, subject to the provisions of this section and to the following provisions of this Part of this Act, the "nearest relative" means the person first described in subsection (1) of this section who is for the time being surviving, relatives of the whole blood being preferred to relatives of the same description of the half-blood, and the elder or eldest of two or more relatives described in any paragraph of that subsection being preferred to the other or others of those relatives regardless of sex.

(4) Where the person who, under subsection (3) of this section would be the nearest relative of a patient—

(a) is not ordinarily resident within the United Kingdom; or
(b) being the husband or wife of the patient, is permanently separated from the patient, either by agreement or under an order of a court, or has deserted or has been deserted by the patient for a period which has not come to an end; or
(c) not being the husband, wife, father or mother of the patient, is for the time being under eighteen years of age; or
(d) is a man against whom an order divesting him of authority over the patient has been made under section thirty-eight of the Sexual Offences Act 1956 (which relates to incest with a girl under eighteen) and has not been rescinded,

the nearest relative of the patient shall be ascertained as if that person were dead.

(5) In this section "adoption order" means an order for the adoption of any person made under Part I of the Adoption Act 1958, or any previous enactment relating to the adoption of children, or any corresponding enactment of the Parliament of Northern Ireland, and "court" includes a court in Scotland or Northern Ireland.

(6) In this section "husband" and "wife" include a person who is living with the patient as the patient's husband or wife, as the case may be (or, if the patient is for the time being an in-patient in a hospital, was so living until the patient was admitted), and has been or had been so living for a period of not less than six months; but a person shall not be treated by virtue of this subsection as the nearest relative of a married patient unless the husband or wife of the patient is disregarded by virtue of paragraph (b) of subsection (4) of this section.

Children and young persons in care of local authority.

Section 50. In any case where the rights and powers of a parent of a patient, being a child or a young person, are vested in a local authority or other person by virtue of—

(a) section twenty-four of the Children and Young Persons Act 1969 (which relates to the powers and duties of local authorities with respect to persons committed to their care in pursuance of that Act);
(b) section three of the Children Act 1948 (which relates to children in respect of whom parental rights have been assumed under section 2 of that Act); or
(c) section seventeen of the Social Work (Scotland) Act 1968 (which makes corresponding provision for Scotland),

that authority or person shall be deemed to be the nearest relative of the patient in preference to any person except the patient's husband or wife (if any) and except, in a case where the said rights and powers are vested in a local authority by virtue of subsection (2) of the said section three, or subsection (2) of the said section seventeen any parent of the patient not being a person on whose account the resolution mentioned in that subsection was passed.

Nearest relative of infant under guardianship, etc.

Section 51.—(1) Where a patient who has not attained the age of eighteen years—

(a) is, by virtue of an order made by a court in the exercise of jurisdiction (whether under any enactment or otherwise) in respect of the guardianship of infants (including an order under section thirty-eight of the Sexual Offences Act 1956), or by virtue of a deed or will executed by his father or mother, under the guardianship of a person not being his nearest relative under the foregoing provisions of this Act, or is under the joint guardianship of two persons of whom one is such a person as aforesaid; or
(b) is, by virtue of an order made by a court in the exercise of such jurisdiction as aforesaid or in matrimonial proceedings, or by virtue of a separation agreement between his father and mother, in the custody of any such person,

the person or persons having the guardianship or custody of the patient shall, to the exclusion of any other person, be deemed to be his nearest relative.

(2) Subsection (4) of section forty-nine of this Act shall apply in relation to a person who is, or who is one of the persons, deemed to be the nearest relative of a patient by virtue of this section as it applies in relation to a person who would be the nearest relative under subsection (3) of that section.

(3) A patient shall be treated for the purposes of this section as being in the custody of another person if he would be in that other person's custody apart from section thirty-four of this Act.

(4) In this section "court" includes a court in Scotland or Northern Ireland, and "enactment" includes an enactment of the Parliament of Northern Ireland.

Appendix: Form 6

MENTAL HEALTH ACT 1959

Application by a Mental Welfare Officer for Admission for Treatment (Section 26)

(1) Name and address of hospital or mental nursing home

TO THE MANAGERS OF (¹)

_____

(2) Name and address of applicant

1. I(²)_____of_____

_____hereby apply for the admission of

(3) Name and address of patient

(³)_____of_____

_____to the above-named hospital for

treatment in accordance with Part IV of the Mental Health Act 1959, as a patient suffering from

(4) Insert mental illness, severe subnormality, subnormality and/or psychopathic disorder

(4)_____

(5) Name of local social services authority

2. I am an officer of (⁵)_____appointed to act as a mental welfare officer for the purposes of the Act.

3. (*This section should be deleted if no consultation has taken place*)

(6) See definition of nearest relative at end of form

(a) I have consulted_____

of_____

who to the best of my knowledge and belief is the patient's nearest relative (⁶) within the meaning of the Act.

OR

(b) I have consulted_____

of_____

who has been authorised by the County Court for_____

to exercise the functions of the patient's nearest relative under the Act.

OR

(c) I have consulted_____

of_____

who has been authorised by_____

who to the best of my knowledge and belief is the patient's nearest relative within the meaning of the Act, to exercise the functions of the patient's nearest relative under the Act.

AND

she/he has not notified me or the local social services ~~health~~ authority by whom I am appointed that

she/he objects to this application being made.

4. (*This section should be deleted if consultation has taken place*)

Delete the TWO statements which do not apply

(a) I have been unable to ascertain who is this patient's nearest relative within the meaning of the Act.

OR

(b) To the best of my knowledge and belief this patient has no nearest relative within the meaning of the Act.

OR

(c) In my opinion it is not reasonably practicable / would involve unreasonable delay before making this application to

consult_____of_____

_____who to the best of my knowledge and belief is

this patient's nearest relative within the meaning of the Act

authorised to exercise the functions of this patient's nearest relative under the Act.

[P.T.O

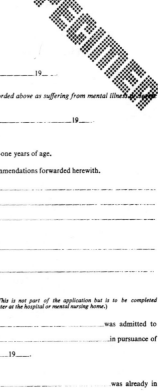

5. I last saw the patient on...19___ ...

6. (*This section is to be deleted if the patient is recorded above as suffering from mental illness or severe subnormality*)

    (a) The patient's date of birth is_____19____.

Delete (a) or (h)

    OR (if the exact age is not known)

    (b) I believe the patient to be under twenty-one years of age.

7. This application is founded on the medical recommendations forwarded herewith.

(7) If neither of the medical practitioners who have made the recommendations had previous acquaintance with the patient the applicant should state here why it is not practicable to obtain a recommendation from a practitioner having such acquaintance

8. ([7]) ....

....

....

             Signed ....

             Date ....

RECORD OF ADMISSION (*This is not part of the application but is to be completed later at the hospital or mental nursing home.*)

(8) Name of patient

  (a) ([8])..was admitted to

(9) Name of hospital or mental nursing home

  ([9])..in pursuance of

this application on...19____.

Delete (a) or (b)

OR

  (b) ([8])...was already in

  ([9])...on the date of

this application, and the application was received by me on behalf of the managers on

....19____.

          Signed ....

                on behalf of the managers

          Date ....

MENTAL HEALTH ACT 1959

Definition of Relative and Nearest Relative

Definition of relative and nearest relative

Section 49.—(1) In this Part of this Act "relative", means any of the following, that is to say—
(a) husband or wife;
(b) son or daughter;
(c) father;
(d) mother;
(e) brother or sister;
(f) grandparent;
(g) grandchild;
(h) uncle or aunt;
(i) nephew or niece.

(2) In deducing relationships for the purpose of this section, an adopted person shall be treated as the child of the person or persons by whom he was adopted and not as the child of any other person; and subject as aforesaid, any relationship of the half-blood shall be treated as a relationship of the whole blood, and an illegitimate person shall be treated as the legitimate child of his mother.

(3) In this Part of this Act, subject to the provisions of this section and to the following provisions of this Part of this Act, the "nearest relative" means the person first described in subsection (1) of this section who is for the time being surviving, relatives of the whole blood being preferred to relatives of the same description of the half-blood, and the elder or eldest of two or more relatives described in any paragraph of that subsection being preferred to the other or others of those relatives regardless of sex.

(4) Where the person who, under subsection (3) of this section would be the nearest relative of a patient—
(a) is not ordinarily resident within the United Kingdom; or
(b) being the husband or wife of the patient, is permanently separated from the patient, either by agreement or under an order of a court, or has deserted or has been deserted by the patient for a period which has not come to an end; or
(c) not being the husband, wife, father or mother of the patient, is for the time being under eighteen years of age; or
(d) is a man against whom an order divesting him of authority over the patient has been made under section thirty-eight of the Sexual Offences Act 1956 (which relates to incest with a girl under eighteen) and has not been rescinded,
the nearest relative of the patient shall be ascertained as if that person were dead.

(5) In this section "adoption order" means an order for the adoption of any person made under Part I of the Adoption Act 1958, or any previous enactment relating to the adoption of children, or any corresponding enactment of the Parliament of Northern Ireland, and "court" includes a court in Scotland or Northern Ireland.

(6) In this section "husband" and "wife" include a person who is living with the patient as the patient's husband or wife, as the case may be (or, if the patient is for the time being as an in-patient in a hospital, was so living until the patient was admitted), and has been or had been so living for a period of not less than six months; but a person shall not be treated by virtue of this subsection as the nearest relative of a married patient unless the husband or wife of the patient is disregarded by virtue of paragraph (b) of subsection (4) of this section.

Children and young persons in care of local authority

Section 50. In any case where the rights and powers of a parent of a patient, being a child or a young person, are vested in a local authority or other person by virtue of—
(a) section twenty-four of the Children and Young Persons Act 1969 (which relates to the powers and duties of local authorities with respect to persons committed to their care in pursuance of that Act);
(b) section seventy-nine of the Children and Young Persons (Scotland) Act 1937 which makes corresponding provision in Scotland); or
(c) section three of the Children Act 1948 (which relates to children in respect of whom parental rights have been assumed under section 2 of that Act),
that authority or persons shall be deemed to be the nearest relative of the patient in preference to any person except the patient's husband or wife (if any) and except, in a case where the said rights and powers are vested in a local authority by virtue of subsection (2) of the said section three, any parent of the patient not being a person on whose account the resolution mentioned in that subsection was passed.

Nearest relative of infant under guardianship, etc.

Section 51.—(1) Where a patient who has not attained the age of eighteen years—
(a) is, by virtue of an order made by a court in the exercise of jurisdiction (whether under any enactment or otherwise) in respect of the guardianship of infants (including an order under section thirty-eight of the Sexual Offences Act 1956), or by virtue of a deed or will executed by his father or mother, under the guardianship of a person not being his nearest relative under the foregoing provisions of this Act, or is under the joint guardianship of two persons of whom one is such a person as aforesaid; or
(b) is, by virtue of an order made by a court in the exercise of such jurisdiction as aforesaid or in matrimonial proceedings, or by virtue of a separation agreement between his father and mother, in the custody of any such person,
the person or persons having the guardianship or custody of the patient shall, to the exclusion of any other person, be deemed to be his nearest relative.

(2) Subsection (4) of section forty-nine of this Act shall apply in relation to a person who is, or who is one of the persons, deemed to be the nearest relative of a patient by virtue of this section as it applies in relation to a person who would be the nearest relative under subsection (3) of that section.

(3) A patient shall be treated for the purposes of this section as being in the custody of another person if he would be in that other person's custody apart from section thirty-four of this Act.

(4) In this section "court" includes a court in Scotland or Northern Ireland, and "enactment" includes an enactment of the Parliament of Northern Ireland.

Form 12

MENTAL HEALTH ACT 1959

Report Barring Discharge by Nearest Relative (Section 48 (2))

(1) Name of hospital or mental nursing home in which patient is liable to be detained

TO THE MANAGERS OF(¹)

I hereby report, for the purposes of Section 48(2) of the Mental Health Act 1959, that I am of the

(2) Name of patient

opinion that (²)

would be likely to act in a manner dangerous to other persons or to himself. / herself.

Signed ....
Responsible Medical Officer

Date ....19......

(3) Time and date

To be completed on behalf of the managers

This report was received by me on behalf of the managers at(³)..

on..19......

Signed ....

Date ....19......

The patient's nearest relative, whose notice of intention to order the patient's discharge was received

at(³)..on..19......,

was informed of this report on..19......

Signed ....
On behalf of the managers.

Date ....19......

MENTAL HEALTH ACT, 1959

Form 2

Emergency Application for Admission for Observation
(Section 29)

(1) Name and address of hospital or mental nursing home

TO THE MANAGERS OF (¹)...

....

(2) Name and address of applicant

1. I (²).. of ....

....hereby apply for the admission of

(3) Name and address of patient

(³).. of ....

....to the above-named hospital for observation in accordance with Part IV of the Mental Health Act, 1959.

(4) State relationship (see section 49 overleaf)

2. (a) I am a relative of the patient within the meaning of the Act, being the patient's (⁴)..............

....

Delete (a) or (b)

OR

(5) Name of local social services authority

(b) I am an officer of (⁵)...
appointed to act as a mental welfare officer for the purposes of the Act.

3. I last saw the patient on ....19......

4. In my opinion it is of urgent necessity for the patient to be admitted and detained under Section 25 of the Act, and compliance with the requirements of the Act relating to applications for admission other than emergency applications would involve undesirable delay.

5. This application is founded on the medical recommendation forwarded herewith.

(6) If the medical practitioner who has made the recommendation had no previous acquaintance with the patient, the applicant should state here why it is not practicable to obtain a recommendation from a practitioner having such acquaintance

6. (⁶)...

....

....

....

....

Signed..

Date ....

RECORD OF ADMISSION
(This is not part of the application, but is to be completed later at the hospital or mental nursing home.)

(7) Name of patient

(a) (⁷)...was admitted to

(⁸)...in pursuance of

this application at (⁹)...........................on..........................19..........

Delete (a) or (b)

OR

(b) (⁷)...was already an in-patient

(8) Name of hospital or mental nursing home

in (⁸) ....

on the date of this application and the application was received by me on behalf of the managers

(9) Time and date

at (⁹)...........................on..........................19..........

Signed..
on behalf of the managers

Date ....

MENTAL HEALTH ACT, 1959

Definition of Relative

Section 49.—(1) In this Part of this Act "relative", means any of the following, that is to say—

(a) husband or wife;
(b) son or daughter;
(c) father;
(d) mother;
(e) brother or sister;
(f) grandparent;
(g) grandchild;
(h) uncle or aunt;
(i) nephew or niece.

(2) In deducing relationships for the purposes of this section, an adopted person shall be treated as the child of the person or persons by whom he was adopted and not as the child of any other person; and subject as aforesaid, any relationship of the half-blood shall be treated as a relationship of the whole blood, and an illegitimate person shall be treated as the legitimate child of his mother.

*   *   *   *   *

(5) In this section "adoption order" means an order for the adoption of any person made under Part I of the Adoption Act, 1958, or any previous enactment relating to the adoption of children, or any corresponding enactment of the Parliament of Northern Ireland, and "court" includes a court in Scotland or Northern Ireland.

(6) In this section "husband" and "wife" include a person who is living with the patient as the patient's husband or wife, as the case may be (or, if the patient is for the time being an in-patient in a hospital, was so living until the patient was admitted), and has been or had been so living for a period of not less than six months; but a person shall not be treated by virtue of this subsection as the nearest relative of a married patient unless the husband or wife of the patient is disregarded by virtue of paragraph (b) of subsection (4) of this section.

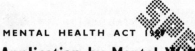

MENTAL HEALTH ACT 1959   Form 7B

Guardianship Application by Mental Welfare Officer
(Section 33)

(1) Name of local social services authority

To (¹) ....

(2) Name and address of applicant

1. I (²).. of ....

(3) Name and address of patient

.... hereby apply for the reception of (³) ....
....of ....

(4) Name and address of proposed guardian

.... into the guardianship of (⁴) ....
.... of ....

(5) Insert mental illness, severe subnormality, subnormality and/or psychopathic disorder

in accordance with Part IV of the Mental Health Act 1959, as a patient suffering from (⁵) ....
....

2. I am an officer of (¹)...
appointed to act as a mental welfare officer for the purposes of the Act.

3. (*This section should be deleted if no consultation has taken place.*)

Delete the TWO statements which do not apply.

 (a) I have consulted.. of ....
   who to the best of my knowledge and belief is the patient's nearest relative(⁶) within the meaning of the Act;
 OR
 (b) I have consulted.. of ....
   who has been authorised by the County Court for ....
   to exercise the functions of the patient's nearest relative;
 OR
 (c) I have consulted.. of ....
   who has been authorised by...
   who to the best of my knowledge and belief is the patient's nearest relative within the meaning of the Act, to exercise the function of the patient's nearest relative under the Act,

 AND
 that person has not notified me or the local social services authority by whom I am appointed that he/she objects to this application being made.

(6) See definition of nearest relative overleaf

4. (*This section should be deleted if consultation has taken place.*)

Delete the TWO statements which do not apply.

 (a) I have been unable to ascertain who is this patient's nearest relative within the meaning of the Act;
 OR
 (b) To the best of my knowledge and belief this patient has no nearest relative within the meaning of the Act.
 OR
 (c) In my opinion it is not reasonably practicable / would involve unreasonable delay before making this application to consult
   .... of ....
   who to the best of my knowledge and belief is this patient's nearest relative within the meaning of the Act. / authorised to exercise the functions of this patient's nearest relative under the Act.

5. I last saw the patient on....................................19.........

6. (*This section is to be deleted if the patient is recorded above as suffering from mental illness or severe subnormality.*)

Delete (a) and (b)

 (a) The patient's date of birth is...19.........
 OR (if the exact age is not known)
 (b) I believe the patient to be under the age of twenty-one years.

7. This application is founded on the medical recommendations forwarded herewith.

(7) If neither of the medical practitioners who have made the recommendations had previous acquaintance with the patient, the applicant should state here why it is not practicable to obtain a medical recommendation from a medical practitioner having such acquaintance

8. (⁷) ....
....
....
....
....

       Signed ....
       Date ....

Record of Acceptance (*To be completed on behalf of the local social services authority.*)

This application was accepted by / on behalf of (¹)...
on...19.........

       Signed ....
       Date ....

MENTAL HEALTH ACT 1959

Definition of Relative and Nearest Relative

Definition of relative and nearest relative

Section 49.—(1) In this Part of this Act "relative" means any of the following, that is to say—
(a) husband or wife;
(b) son or daughter;
(c) father;
(d) mother;
(e) brother or sister;
(f) grandparent;
(g) grandchild;
(h) uncle or aunt;
(i) nephew or niece.

(2) In deducing relationships for the purpose of this section, an adopted person shall be treated as the child of the person or persons by whom he was adopted and not as the child of any other person; and subject as aforesaid, any relationship of the half-blood shall be treated as a relationship of the whole blood, and an illegitimate person shall be treated as the legitimate child of his mother.

(3) In this Part of this Act, subject to the provisions of this section and to the following provisions of this Part of this Act, the "nearest relative" means the person first described in subsection (1) of this section who is for the time being surviving, relatives of the whole blood being preferred to relatives of the same description of the half-blood, and the elder or eldest of two or more relatives described in any paragraph of that subsection being preferred to the other or others of those relatives regardless of sex.

(4) Where the person who, under subsection (3) of this section would be the nearest relative of a patient—
(a) is not ordinarily resident within the United Kingdom; or
(b) being the husband or wife of the patient, is permanently separated from the patient, either by agreement or under an order of a court, or has deserted or has been deserted by the patient for a period which has not come to an end; or
(c) not being the husband, wife, father or mother of the patient, is for the time being under eighteen years of age; or
(d) is a man against whom an order divesting him of authority over the patient has been made under section thirty-eight of the Sexual Offences Act 1956 (which relates to incest with a girl under eighteen) and has not been rescinded,
the nearest relative of the patient shall be ascertained as if that person were dead.

(5) In this section "adoption order" means an order for the adoption of any person made under Part I of the Adoption Act 1958, or any previous enactment relating to the adoption of children, or any corresponding enactment of the Parliament of Northern Ireland, and "court" includes a court in Scotland or Northern Ireland.

(6) In this section "husband" and "wife" include a person who is living with the patient as the patient's husband or wife, as the case may be (or, if the patient is for the time being an in-patient in a hospital, was so living until the patient was admitted), and has been or had been so living for a period of not less than six months; but a person shall not be treated by virtue of this subsection as the nearest relative of a married patient unless the husband or wife of the patient is disregarded by virtue of paragraph (b) of subsection (4) of this section.

Children and young persons in care of local authority

Section 50. In any case where the rights and powers of a parent of a patient, being a child or a young person, are vested in a local authority or other person by virtue of—
(a) section twenty-four of the Children and Young Persons Act 1969 (which relates to the powers and duties of local authorities with respect to persons committed to their care in pursuance of that Act);
(b) section three of the Children Act 1948 (which relates to children in respect of whom parental rights have been assumed under section 2 of that Act); or
(c) section seventeen of the Social Work (Scotland) Act 1968 (which makes corresponding provision for Scotland),
that authority or persons shall be deemed to be the nearest relative of the patient in preference to any person except the patient's husband or wife (if any) and except, in a case where the said rights and powers are vested in a local authority by virtue of subsection (2) of the said section three, or subsection (2) of the said section 17, any parent of the patient not being a person on whose account the resolution mentioned in that subsection was passed.

Nearest relative of infant under guardianship, etc.

Section 51.—(1) Where a patient who has not attained the age of eighteen years—
(a) is, by virtue of an order made by a court in the exercise of jurisdiction (whether under any enactment or otherwise) in respect of the guardianship of infants (including an order under section thirty-eight of the Sexual Offences Act 1956), or by virtue of a deed or will executed by his father or mother, under the guardianship of a person not being his nearest relative under the foregoing provisions of this Act, or is under the joint guardianship of two persons of whom one is such a person as aforesaid; or
(b) is, by virtue of an order made by a court in the exercise of such jurisdiction as aforesaid or in matrimonial proceedings, or by virtue of a separation agreement between his father and mother, in the custody of any such person,
the person or persons having the guardianship or custody of the patient shall, to the exclusion of any other person, be deemed to be his nearest relative.

(2) Subsection (4) of section forty-nine of this Act shall apply in relation to a person who is, or who is one of the persons, deemed to be the nearest relative of a patient by virtue of this section as it applies in relation to a person who would be the nearest relative under subsection (3) of that section.

(3) A patient shall be treated for the purposes of this section as being in the custody of another person if he would be in that other person's custody apart from section thirty-four of this Act.

(4) In this section "court" includes a court in Scotland or Northern Ireland, and "enactment" includes an enactment of the Parliament of Northern Ireland.

Form 8A
(HOSPITAL CODE 90-550)

MENTAL HEALTH ACT, 1959

Medical Recommendation for Reception into Guardianship (Section 33)

(1) Name and address of practitioner

1. I (¹)..of...
...., being a registered medical

(2) Name and address of patient

practitioner, recommend that (²)..
of...
be received into guardianship in accordance with Part IV of the Mental Health Act, 1959.

2. I last examined this patient on...19.........

Delete (a) or (b) unless both apply

3. (a) I was acquainted with the patient previously to conducting that examination.

(3) Name of health authority

(b) I have been approved by (³)..
under Section 28 of the Act as having special experience in the diagnosis or treatment of mental disorder.

(4) Insert mental illness, severe subnormality, subnormality and/or psychopathic disorder (see definitions overleaf)

4. In my opinion this patient is suffering from (⁴)..
of a nature or degree which warrants $\frac{his}{her}$ reception into guardianship under the Act. This opinion

(5) Insert clinical description of patient's mental condition

is founded on the following grounds:—(⁵)

....
....
....
....

Delete (i) or (ii) unless both apply

5. I am of the opinion that it is necessary—
(i) in the patient's interest;
(ii) for the protection of other persons;

(6) Reasons why patient cannot appropriately be cared for without powers of guardianship

that $\frac{he}{she}$ should be so received, and my reasons for this opinion are:—(⁶)

....
....
....
....
....

Signed...
Date ....

MENTAL HEALTH ACT, 1959

Definition and Classification of
Mental Disorder

Section 4.—(1) In this Act "mental disorder" means mental illness, arrested or incomplete development of mind, psychopathic disorder, and any other disorder or disability of mind; and "mentally disordered" shall be construed accordingly.

(2) In this Act "severe subnormality" means a state of arrested or incomplete development of mind which includes subnormality of intelligence and is of such a nature or degree that the patient is incapable of living an independent life or of guarding himself against serious exploitation, or will be so incapable when of an age to do so.

(3) In this Act "subnormality" means a state of arrested or incomplete development of mind (not amounting to severe subnormality) which includes subnormality of intelligence and is of a nature or degree which requires or is susceptible to medical treatment or other special care or training of the patient.

(4) In this Act "psychopathic disorder" means a persistent disorder or disability of mind (whether or not including subnormality of intelligence) which results in abnormally aggressive or seriously irresponsible conduct on the part of the patient, and requires or is susceptible to medical treatment.

(5) Nothing in this section shall be construed as implying that a person may be dealt with under this act as suffering from mental disorder, or from any form of mental disorder described in this section by reason only of promiscuity or other immoral conduct.

Appendix: Form 11

MENTAL HEALTH ACT, 1959

(Sections 60 and 61)

_____

REPORT

on the mental condition of

....born on....................19.........

_____

I ....(qualifications)........................
      (FULL NAME)
of..

a registered medical practitioner [*and approved by...

....for the purposes of section 28 of the Mental
Health Act, 1959, as having special experience in the diagnosis or treatment of mental
disorder] have examined this patient.

In my opinion—

    (a)   this patient is suffering from psychopathic disorder within the meaning of the
           Mental Health Act, 1959, and

    (b)   h..... mental disorder is of a nature or degree which warrants the reception
           of the patient into guardianship under that Act.

In case the court should make a guardianship order...

....is willing to receive h..... into guardianship

[*and has been approved by..].

My full medical report is given on the reverse.

Signature..

Date..

* Delete if inappropriate.

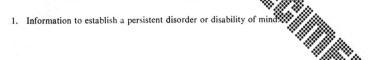

MEDICAL REPORT

1. Information to establish a persistent disorder or disability of mind.

2. Information to establish that the disorder or disability of mind results in abnormally aggressive or seriously irresponsible conduct on the part of the patient.

3. Information to establish that the disorder or disability of mind requires or is susceptible to medical treatment.

4. Reasons for the conclusion that the disorder or disability of mind is of a nature or degree which warrants the reception of the patient into guardianship.

Signature...

Date...

MENTAL HEALTH ACT, 1959

(Section 60 and 61)

_____

REPORT

on the mental condition of

....born on................... ....19............

_____

I...(qualifications)................... ....
   (FULL NAME)

of...

a registered medical practitioner [* and approved by...

....for the purposes of section 28 of the Mental Health Act, 1959, as having special experience in the diagnosis or treatment of mental disorder] have examined this patient.

In my opinion—

(a) this patient is suffering from mental illness within the meaning of the Mental Health Act, 1959 and

(b) h.....mental disorder is of a nature or degree which warrants the detention of the patient in a hospital for medical treatment.

In case the court should make a hospital order, arrangements have been made for the admission of the patient to..
immediately/within 28 days of the order. [*For the reasons given in my report, treatment in a special hospital is recommended.]   [*That hospital is, however, unable to admit h..... before the..

Pending h..... admission to that hospital the managers of...
are willing to receive the patient if the court should give directions under section 64 (1) of the Mental Health Act, 1959, for h..... conveyance to and detention in the last named hospital.]

My full medical report is given on the reverse.

Signature..

Form No. 1303A

Date...

*Delete if inappropriate.

MEDICAL REPORT

1. Information to establish mental illness, including reference to kind of illness and description of symptoms.

2. Reasons for the conclusion that the mental illness is of a nature or degree which warrants the detention of the patient into hospital for medical treatment.

Signature...

Date...

H.M.

Medical Report under Section 72 of the Mental Health Act 1959

SPECIMEN

Name in full (block letters)

Date of birth

If committed in custody to a higher court, the date of committal

Convicted at .... on

Sentenced at .... on

Sentence or order of the court

Offence(s)

..............................days lost on appeal

..............................days unlawfully at large

Date of expiration of sentence

Earliest date of release (if applicable)

I .... (qualifications)
(FULL NAME)
of
a registered medical practitioner [*and approved by
...........................for the purposes of section 28 of the Mental Health Act, 1959, as having special experience in the diagnosis or treatment of mental disorder] have examined this patient.

In my opinion—

    (a) this patient is suffering from mental illness within the meaning of the Mental Health Act, 1959, and

    (b) h.... mental disorder is of a nature or degree which warrants the detention of the patient in a hospital for medical treatment under that Act.

My full medical report is given on the reverse. [*For the reasons there given, if the Secretary of State should give a transfer direction, treatment in a special hospital is recommended.]

Signature

Date

    *Delete if inappropriate.

MEDICAL REPORT

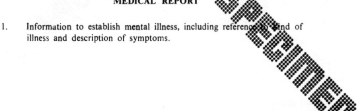

1.   Information to establish mental illness, including reference to kind of illness and description of symptoms.

2.   Reason for the conclusion that the mental illness is of a nature or degree which warrants the detention of the patient into hospital for medical treatment.

Signature...

Date...

H.M. ....

Medical Report under Section 72 of the Mental Health Act, 1959

_____

Name in full (block letters)..

Date of birth ....

If committed in custody to a higher court, the date of committal.....................................

Convicted at ....on...

Sentenced at ....on...

Sentence or order of the court..

Offence (s) ....

..............................days lost on appeal

..............................days unlawfully at large

Date of expiration of sentence..

Earliest date of release (if applicable)..

_____

I...(qualifications)............................
   (FULL NAME)

of...

a registered medical practitioner [*and approved by..

....for the purpose of section 28 of the Mental

Health Act, 1959, as having special experience in the diagnosis or treatment of mental

disorder] have examined this patient.

In my opinion—
   (a) this patient is suffering from severe subnormality within the meaning of the
      Mental Health Act, 1959, and
   (b) h........ mental disorder is of a nature or degree which warrants the detention of
      the patient in a hospital for medical treatment under that Act.

My full medical report is given on reverse. [*For the reasons there given, if the Secretary
of State should give a transfer direction, treatment in a special hospital is recommended.]

Signature ....

Date..

* Delete if inappropriate.

MEDICAL REPORT

1. Information to establish a state of arrested or incomplete development of mind, including subnormality of intelligence.

2. Information to establish that the state of arrested or incomplete development of mind, is of such a nature or degree that the patient is incapable of living an independent life or of guarding himself against serious exploitation.

3. Reasons for the conclusion that the severe subnormality is of a nature or degree which warrants the detention of the patient in hospital for medical treatment.,

Signature........................ ....

Date........ ....

Glossary

Abreaction: A technique employed by some psychotherapists in the treatment of neurosis: its aim is to release repressed emotional conflict by getting the patient to relive the formative experience in imagination. Abreaction can be facilitated by administering small amounts of drugs such as thiopentone or sodium amytal.

Acting out: Reduction of emotional distress by the release of disturbed behaviour that is unconsciously determined and reflects previous unresolved conflicts and attitudes.

Actus reus: Guilty act.

Adlerian: Approach developed by Alfred Adler, who founded his own movement of individual psychology in 1911. He emphasized social factors and the struggle for power.

Affect: Emotion, feeling or mood.

Affective disorders: Group of psychoses characterized by recurring morbid changes of mood, of either depression or mania.

Agnosia: Loss of ability to recognize various stimuli, such as visual, auditory and tactile.

Agraphia: Loss of ability to write.

Alalia: Loss of ability to talk.

Alexia: Loss of ability to read.

Alzheimer's disease: Pre-senile dementia associated with atrophy of the cortex of the brain. It is now thought that senile dementia may also be Alzheimer's disease.

Ambivalence: Contradictory emotional feelings towards an object, e.g. love and hate for the same person. Normal in interpersonal relationships, unless it occurs to a marked degree.

Amnesia: Inability to remember; may be total or partial. Generally hysterical in nature; rarely physically based, but can be related to head injury.

Anorexia: Loss of appetite.

Anorexia nervosa: Persistent loss of appetite, most commonly suffered by young people; of neurotic origin.

Anosmia: Loss of sense of smell.

Aphasia: Loss of ability to express meaning by the use of speech or writing, or of ability to understand spoken or written language.

Apraxia: Inability to manipulate or deal intelligently with objects; caused by brain damage.

Ataxia: Loss or impairment of muscular co-ordination, resulting in an inability to perform accurate voluntary movement.

Athetosis: Slow, writhing, involuntary movements.

Autistic thinking: Mental activity controlled exclusively by the thinker, without reference to external realities.

Autochthonous ideas: Delusional ideas which spring into the mind independently of the train of thought and are alien to the normal mode of thought. Typical of schizophrenia.

Aversion therapy: A type of behaviour therapy used for the treatment of alcoholism and sexual abnormalities. A painful or unpleasant sensation is brought into association with the abnormal behaviour, e.g. vomiting may be induced by apomorphine injections in an alcoholic.

Behaviourism: School of psychology concerned with observable responses in subjects, rather than with internal processes. It stresses objectivity.

Behaviour therapy: Principles of learning theory applied to the treatment of psychiatric disorders; also called behaviour modification and conditioning therapy.

Bestiality: Sexual relationship with animals.

Blocking: Sudden stoppage in the train of thought.

Catatonia: State of profound mental automatism, or absence of voluntary activity, together with a tendency to immobility and negativism.

Chorea: Motor disorder characterized by jerky spasmodic movements. There are two common types: Sydenham's, of rheumatic origin, and Huntington's, an inherited disease.

Clang associations: Associations formed on the basis of rhyme or sound.

Claustrophobia: Morbid dread of confined spaces.

Clinical: Originally applied to bedside observation, but now used generally to describe techniques of observation and examination for diagnostic purposes.

Cognition: Knowing; thought processes.

Coma: A state of deep unconsciousness.

Complex: A group of repressed ideas active in the unconscious.

Conation: Doing, acting, behaviour.

Conditioning: Ways in which human beings and animals can be systematically taught to respond in a particular way to some form of stimulus. In the classical experiment Pavlov conditioned a dog to salivate by giving it food at the same time as a bell was rung; after a period of conditioning the dog still salivated when the bell was rung but no food provided.

Confabulation: Fabrications to fill memory gaps.

Congenital: Conditions present at birth.

Coprolalia: Utterance of obscene words or phrases.

Couvade syndrome: Psychogenic disorder that affects husbands during their wives' pregnancies or child-bearing; similar to morning sickness or labour pains.

Déjà vu: Sense of familiarity. The sensation that one is seeing something one has previously seen.

Delirium: State of clouded consciousness with confusion and disorientation, often due to an acute febrile illness, or the action of drugs on the brain.

Delusion: False belief which is held with conviction in the face of contrary evidence and which is unmodifiable by appeals to reason or logic that would be appropriate to other persons of the same religious or cultural background.

Dementia: Irreversible impairment of intellectual ability, memory and personality, due to permanent damage or disease of the brain.

Depersonalization: State in which the individual experiences a loss of his own identity or reality.

Derealization: Feeling that the environment is unreal; usually occurs with depersonalization.

Diagnosis: Deduction of the nature of an illness from its history, symptoms, and the special investigations made by the diagnostician.

Dipsomania: Recurrent urge to consume alcohol until intoxication.

Double bind: Term referring to incompatible, contradictory emotional demands, typically a mother's demands of her child, from which there is no escape, other than withdrawal into a psychotic state; a childhood experience might, for example, later lead to the development of schizophrenia.

Down's Syndrome: A condition caused by a chromosomal defect. Also known as mongolism.

Durham test: Refers to the ruling of the US Court of Appeals in 1954 that the accused is not criminally responsible if his unlawful act was the product of mental disease or mental defect.

Dysarthria: Impairment of speech or articulation due to disease directly or indirectly affecting the muscles of speech.

Dyslexia: Inability to read at a level appropriate to the individual's age and intelligence, resulting from a mental or neurological disorder.

Echolalia: Repetition of the words or phrases of another person.

Echopraxia: Repetition of the acts of another person.

ECT: Electroconvulsive therapy. The patient, while under the effects of an anaesthetic and muscle relaxant, is subjected to electric charges which induce an artificial fit.

Empathy: Occurs when an observer is able to enter into the thoughts and feelings of the patient and establish a good contact.

Encephalitis: Inflammation of the brain.

Endocrine gland: Ductless gland which pours its secretions directly into the blood or other circulating fluids.

Enuresis: Incontinence of urine.

Epilepsy: Episodic abnormality of the brain function with loss of consciousness, which may or may not be associated with spasms and contractions of the muscles.

Fetishism: Sexual arousal by objects not generally regarded as sexually stimulating.

Flagellation: Whipping, may be the source of erotic pleasure.

Flight of ideas: Succession of thoughts or utterances with no apparent rational connection, though closer observation may reveal links, however tenuous, such as a similarity between the last word of one sentence and the first word of the next. Clang associations also occur. Typical of hypomania and mania.

Flooding: A form of treatment where the patient is exposed to the situation which makes him anxious until he is able to face it without anxiety.

Folie à deux: Sharing of delusions by two closely associated people, such as husband and wife, one of whom suffers from a paranoid illness and eventually induces similar delusions in the other.

Fugue: State of alteration of consciousness combined with an impulse to wander. Occurs in hysteria and some kinds of severe epilepsy.

Ganser syndrome: A condition in which the patient gives approximate answers to questions, e.g. answering 'Five' when asked the number of legs of a cow. A manifestation of hysteria, or malingering.

GPI: General paralysis of the insane, a disease of the nervous system caused by syphilis.

Group psychotherapy: Group meetings of patients with a therapist. The object is to achieve mental purgation.

Hallucination: False perception lacking external basis or stimulation.

Hormone: Substance produced by an endocrine gland.

Huntington's chorea: Hereditary disease of the nervous system characterized by jerky movements and a progressive dementia.

Hypnagogic: The drowsy state just before falling asleep. Thoughts and mental images frequently take on the character of hallucination.

Hypnosis: Artificially induced state similar in many respects to sleep but specifically characterized by exaggerated suggestibility and the continuance of contact or rapport with the hypnotist. Sometimes used as a form of psychotherapy.

Hypochondria: Exaggerated or obsessive attention to and anxiety about one's health.

Hypomania: Milder form of mania.

Iatrogenic: Illness caused by treatment.

Ideas of reference: Unfounded ideas that other people are referring to one in their speech, writing and gestures.

Idiopathic: Pathological condition in which no cause can be discovered.

Illusion: False perception with external stimulation. Illusion should be distinguished from hallucination, but like it may involve many of the senses. Illusion is more common at night and generally occurs in a state of altered consciousness.

Incongruity of affect: Disharmony between the patient's emotional state and accompanying thoughts; may be a feature of schizophrenia.

Industrial therapy: Work used as treatment helping the patient to develop self-respect and the ability to operate under factory conditions.

Kleptomania: Morbid impulse to steal.

Knight's move thinking: Symbolically, from the knight's move in chess, which consists of moving the piece two squares in one direction and then one square to the left or the right. Tangential thinking.

Korsakoff's psychosis: One consequence of chronic alcoholism in which multiple neuritis, memory loss and confabulation occur.

Libido: Sexual drive.

Logorrhoea: Rapid and voluble speech.

McNaghten Rules: In 1843 Daniel McNaghten shot and killed Alexander Drummond, private secretary to Sir Robert Peel. McNaghten suffered from delusions of persecution, and was found not guilty. Following this case a debate in the House of Lords led to the formulation of the McNaghten Rules. The rules state that in order to establish a defence on grounds of insanity the following conditions must be fulfilled:
(1) it must be proved that at the time of committing the act the accused was labouring under such a defect of reason from disease of the mind as not to know the nature and quality of the act he was doing, or, if he did know what he was doing, he did not know that it was wrong; (2) if the accused commits an act by reason of delusion the degree of responsibility is based on the justification which the delusion would provide if it were true; (3) everybody is presumed sane until the contrary is proved.

Masochism: Obtaining sexual pleasure through suffering physical pain.

Menarche: Beginning of menstrual function; indicates puberty and the start of the reproductive period in the female.

Menopause: The time of life when menstruation stops; the 'change of life'.

Mens rea: Malice aforethought or guilty mind. A bare intent, however criminal, is not punishable unless followed by a criminal act.

Milieu: Immediate environment, physical and social, but in psychology usually with emphasis upon the latter.

Mood: An affective condition or attitude enduring for some time, characterized by particular emotions, e.g. an irritable mood or a cheerful mood.

Mutism: State of being mute, without the power of speech.

Narcoanalysis: Abreaction with a narcotic such as sodium amytal.

Neologism: Invention and use of new words, often devoid of meaning.

Neurasthenia: Pathological weakness characterized by physical and mental fatigue.

Neuritis: Pain in the distribution of a nerve; inflammation of a nerve.

Neuroses: Disorders of the personality in which instinctive and emotional difficulties become expressed in mental and physical symptoms.

Neurosyphilis: Syphilis involving the nervous system.

Occupational therapy: Therapeutic approach by means of purposeful occupation.

Oedipus complex: Desire of the son to displace his father and possess his mother.

Operant conditioning: Strengthening of a stimulus—response association achieved by following the response with a reinforcing stimulus.

Othello syndrome: Morbid sexual jealousy.

Over-valued idea: Emotionally charged idea which tends to dominate the thoughts.

Paranoia: Psychosis characterized by fixed and systematized delusion; personality is well preserved and there are no hallucinations.

Paranoid: Persistent, unjustified feelings of persecution.

Passivity feelings: A feeling of being under some outside control.

Pathological jealousy: Certain degrees of jealousy in, for example, a husband or wife may be normal, but if one constantly suspects the other of infidelity without grounds, it is considered a morbid condition.

Pathology: Branch of biological or medical science which concerns itself with abnormal and diseased conditions. The term is used to mean underlying disease, as in the expression 'pathological lying'.

Phobia: Dread or uncontrollable fear of some object or situation.

Primary delusion: A delusion arising without cause. Often the first sign of schizophrenia.

Projection: Defence mechanism by which one judges others by oneself.

Psychodrama: Form of group therapy involving the dramatic staging of patients' problems by fellow patients or members of the therapeutic team.

Psychotherapy: Psychological method of treatment of mental disorders.

Rapport: Feeling of emotional contact with another person.

Rationalization: Mental mechanism which devises reasons to justify behaviour that is actually based on other motives.

Reflex: Automatic, involuntary response to a stimulus.

Repression: Psychological process which eliminates unacceptable impulses or ideas from consciousness.

Retardation: Slow speech and behaviour observed in depressive illness. All movements may be retarded and every action seems to take an enormous effort.

Ritual: System of ceremonies or procedures carried out compulsively and without variation.

Sadism: Sexual perversion in which pleasure is obtained by inflicting pain.

Senescence: Growing old. The degenerative changes which begin relatively early in life but become more marked as old age approaches.

Sibling: Children with one or both parents in common; brothers and sisters.

Somatic disorders: Disorders of the body, excluding and contrasting with nervous disorders.

Somnambulism: Walking and carrying out other complex activities while asleep.

Stupor: An unconscious, unresponsive state.

Syndrome: A complex combination of the various symptoms of a disease.

Therapeutic community: A social organization in which a patient can derive benefit from being part of a whole. Certain basic principles are involved: democracy, permissiveness, communalism and the confrontation of reality.

Therapeutics: The branch of medicine concerned with the treatment of disorders.

Tic: Spasmodic or sudden twitch, generally of one of the facial or head muscles; as a rule it originates in some psychoneurotic disturbance.

Toxic psychosis: Mental disorder due to the action of toxins, including drugs.

Transference: Term used by psychoanalysts to describe the patient's development of an emotional attitude, negative or positive, towards the analyst.

Trauma: An injury or wound, most frequently physical or structural, which precipitates an emotional shock producing more or less enduring mental disturbance.

Unconscious: Part of the mind not accessible to conscious thought.

Word-salad: Incomprehensible speech containing nonsense, jargon and neologisms. Typical of schizophrenia.

Index

178 *Index*